MW00718799

American Sock Knitting

Beth Moriarty

 **Planet Purl Press**

Book Design: Beth Moriarty and
Erin Janes Brooks
Project Photography: Beth Moriarty
Text Editor: Cavan Hallman
Technical Editor: Kate Atherley

 Planet Purl Press
PO Box 149524
Orlando, FL 32814, USA
www.PlanetPurl.com

Printed in China through Asia Pacific
Offset

Library of Congress Cataloging-in-
Publication Data

Moriarty, Beth, 1956-
American Sock Knitting: Celebrating
America's Beauty Through Handknit
Socks/ Beth Moriarty

1st ed. - Planet Purl Press, 2013.

96p.: illus.; 9mm - (Knitting patterns, travel
in the United States, American regional
cooking). - Includes index.

ISBN 978-0-9859371-5-7 (pbk.)

Library of Congress Control Number:
2013905788

Acknowledgments

AMERICAN *Sock Knitting* is the work of a dozen talented sock designers. Many thanks to our contributors who were inspired by their love for the land we call home. Thanks as well to Natalie at DreamWeaverYarns.com who helped provide contest prizes for the selected patterns.

It takes a team to bring any book to completion, and this was no exception. Thanks to my models, Olivia and Patricia Short, and Elisha Charpentier, for having great legs and being so patient while holding weird positions to show off the socks. Many thanks to technical editor, Kate Atherley, who provided a highly skilled and much needed second pair of eyes. Thanks to my text editor, Cavan Hallman, who polished my grammar and syntax.

Thanks to Erin Janes Brooks, for starting me down this publishing road and nurturing the tiny idea that became PlanetPurl.com. She gets the credit for the evolution of Planet Purl Press. Never underestimate the value of someone assuring you that some task they want you to undertake will be "easy!"

Of course, thanks to all the supporters of Planet Purl who keep our online family going. Your enthusiasm for our books will help ensure that Planet Purl sticks around as a resource for knitters and crocheters everywhere.

And last but definitely not least, my husband Michael Langan — who I teasingly call "Mr. PurlQueen" — without whom I would still be an unhappy lawyer rather than a happy knitter. There are no words to tell you what you mean to me, my love.

I hope sock knitters enjoy this second publication from Planet Purl Press. I had a lot of fun putting it together and am already hard at work on the rest of this series with AMERICAN *Gift Knitting* up next!

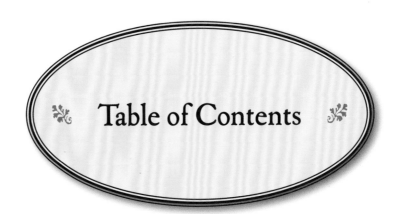

Table of Contents

Patterns

Classic American Recipes

America the Beautiful

Extras

To sock knitters everywhere,
may your toes always be warm
and your ankles never baggy

Welcome

AMERICAN *Sock Knitting* was born from a contest on my website, PlanetPurl.com, inviting sock knitters to put their considerable talents to work designing socks inspired by their favorite places in the United States.

Sock knitting is almost an obsession in the U.S. Maybe it's because we all have feet, or because socks make a great gift with little worry about size, or because the work-in-progress fits handily in a purse. Whatever the reason, American sock knitters and their friends and families are sporting some very cool foot coverings!

Choosing a dozen socks was a difficult job. To bring the project count to a baker's dozen, I designed a sock inspired by my home in the mountains of North Carolina. These thirteen designs celebrate the natural beauty and stunning variety of our country. From deserts to oceans, mountains to country gardens, American sock knitters are definitely inspired by the world around them. I hope you will be, too.

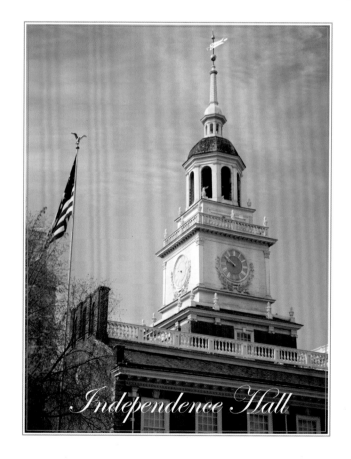

Independence Hall

Statue of Liberty

Northeast

*I*t's natural that the Northeast is our first section of the book — there are more feet in this region than in any of the others! When most of us think "Northeast" we think about the mega-cities, factories and mills, but the area's residents know that some of the country's most beautiful scenery year-round is just a hop, skip and jump from the hustle and bustle of New York City, Boston, Philadelphia, and other major population centers.

During the summer months, locals flock to the region's beaches and coastal towns. From the boardwalk of Atlantic City, to the Victorian charm of Cape May, to the glamor of the Hamptons, Northeastern beaches have wide swaths of sand without the South's stifling humidity.

For the sailing crowd, the Northeast is *the* place to be. One of my favorite places is Newport, Rhode Island, home to America's Cup yacht racing. The historic waterfront looks like something plucked right from the late 18th century. In addition to some of the best chowder and seafood you'll ever taste, if you like cranberries — and I love them— you'll find cranberry everything, from muffins, pancakes and scones to cranberry fudge.

Fall draws visitors in droves to experience premier leaf-peeping as autumn turns the trees to works of art in reds and golds. Tourists seeking a relaxed view can drive the scenic highways, staying in the region's acclaimed bed and breakfasts. Seeking a more active and up-close-and-personal view? Pull on your boots and hike some of the 1100+ miles of the Appalachian Trail that crosses Maine, New Hampshire, Vermont, Massachusetts, Connecticut, New York, New Jersey and Pennsylvania. You can leave Manhattan and be on the trail in an hour.

History buffs will love the Northeast. Almost half of the country's National Historic Landmarks are located in the region. Records of early America are written across the land — prehistoric archaeological sites, Plymouth Rock, Independence Hall, John Brown's Home and Gravesite, and the courthouse where Susan B. Anthony was tried and convicted of attempting to vote — each presents vivid reminders of the region's rich past.

❧ Winter Chases Fall ❧

One thing I missed growing up in Florida was the change of seasons. Sure, the cypress trees turn brown and all their needles fall off and get stuck in your hair, socks, and your dog's coat, but I don't think that counts.

It's easy to understand the leaf-peeping mania that sends people in droves to the Northeast every fall. A light dusting of snow is just the icing on the cake! Massachusetts designer Susan Todhunter pays homage to nature's most brilliant season with these autumnal beauties, perfectly frosted with snowy toes and heels.

Sock Type: Toe up

Finished Sizes: Women's S (M, L): Foot circumference: 5¼ (6¾, 8)" (13 [17, 20]cm); leg length from ankle: 4½ (6, 7½)" (11.5 [15, 19]cm); foot length 7 (8½, 9½)" (17.5 [20, 22.5]cm) or to fit (unstretched)

Project Gauge: 30 stitches and 52 rounds = 4" (10cm) in stockinette stitch with MC; 29 stitches and 48 rounds = 4" (10cm) in *Chase Slipped Stitch Mosaic*

Shopping List
Cascade *Fixation* (98.3% cotton/1.7% elastic; 100 yards/91m); 2 skeins Natural #8176 (MC)
Valley Yarns *Franklin* (75% wool, 25% nylon, 450 yards/412m); 1 skein Indian Summer (CC)
Size US 1 (2.25mm) circular needles, 2 sets
Size US 2 (2.75mm) circular needles, 2 sets
Tapestry needle

Stitch Guide
Chase Slipped Stitch Mosaic Pattern (multiple of 5 stitches)
Rounds 1-2: With CC, *k4, sl1; repeat from * to end.
Rounds 3-4: With MC, *sl1, k4; repeat from * to end.
Rounds 5-6: With CC, k1, *sl1, k4; repeat from * to last 4 stitches, sl1, k3.
Rounds 7-8: With MC, k2, *sl1, k4; repeat from * to last 3 stitches, sl1, k2.
Rounds 9-10: With CC, k3, *sl1, k4; repeat from * to last 2 stitches, sl1, k1.

Rounds 11-12: With MC, *k4, sl1; repeat from * to end.
Rounds 13-14: With CC, *sl1, k4; repeat from * to end.
Rounds 15-16: With MC, k1, *sl1, k4; repeat from * to last 4 stitches, sl1, k3.
Rounds 17-18: With CC, k2, *sl1, k4; repeat from * to last 3 stitches, sl1, k2.
Rounds 19-20: With MC, k3, *sl1, k4; repeat from * to last 2 stitches, sl1, k1.
Repeat these 20 rounds for pattern.

4x1 Rib (Multiple of 5 stitches)
Every round: *K4, *p1, repeat from * to end.

M1-L − Make One Left
With tip of left needle, lift the strand that runs between the stitch just worked and the next stitch, from front to back; knit into the back.

M1-R - Make One Right
With tip of left needle, lift the strand that runs between the stitch just worked and the next stitch, from back to front; knit into the front.

Instructions
Toe
With the larger needles and MC, using either Judy's Magic Cast On or Turkish Cast On, CO 16 (18, 20) stitches. 8 (9, 10) stitches on each needle. Needle 1 begins round. Work one round in stockinette stitch. Note: Work toe in MC only.
Round 1: Needle 1: *k1, M1-R, work until one stitch remains, M1-L, k1; repeat from * to end; Needle 2: repeat from * to end. 4 stitches increased.
Round 2: Work even.
Repeat these two rounds until there are 20 (25, 30) stitches on each needle. Work one round even.

Instep
With both MC and CC, work *Chase Slipped Stitch Mosaic Pattern* until instep measures 6 (7½, 8½)" (15 [19, 21.5]cm), or 1" (2.5cm) less than desired length from toe to back of heel, ending with two rounds CC.

Short row heel
Note: Heel is worked in stockinette with MC, back and forth on one needle.
Hold sock with Needle 1 facing. Knit side is RS.
Row 1 (RS): Knit across Needle 1 to last stitch, w&t.
Row 2 (WS): Purl back to last stitch on Needle 1, w&t.
Row 3: Knit to last unwrapped stitch on Needle 1, w&t.
Row 4: Purl back to last unwrapped stitch, w&t.
Repeat rows 3-4, five (seven, eight) times. 6 (7, 10) wrapped stitches at each end of Needle 1.

Joining heel
With RS facing and MC, work across remaining stitches on Needle 1, knitting wraps with wrapped stitches; work across Needle 2 in *Chase Slipped Stitch Mosaic Pattern.*

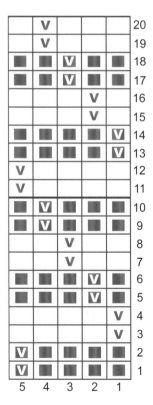

Chase Slipped Stitch Mosaic Pattern

| V | Slip stitch wyib

Turning the heel

Hold sock with Needle 1 facing and work with MC only.
Note: Wraps on first row will be facing the wrong way and
a little awkward to work; knit them together with wrapped
stitches as usual.

Row 1 (RS): Knit to first wrapped stitch, work wrapped
stitch together with its wrap, w&t.

Row 2 (WS): Purl to first wrapped stitch, work wrapped
stitch together with its wrap, w&t.

Row 3: Knit to first wrapped stitch, work wrapped stitch
together with its wraps, w&t.

Row 4: Purl to first wrapped stitch, work wrapped stitch
together with its wraps, w&t.

Repeat row 3-4 until first and last stitches on Needle 1 are
double-wrapped.

Next round: With RS facing and MC, work across Needle 1
in stockinette stitch, working wraps with wrapped stitches,
then work across Needle 2, maintaining *Chase Slipped
Stitch Mosaic Pattern.*

Leg

With Needle 1 and CC, resume working *Chase Slipped
Stitch Mosaic Pattern* circularly, with next round in
sequence, working wrap together with first stitch on Needle
1. Work even until sock leg measures approximately 3½
(5, 6½)" (9 [13, 17]cm) from heel turning (at center of heel),
ending with round 6 and CC.

Ribbing

With smaller needles and MC, work ½" (1.25cm) in *4x1 rib*.
BO loosely in rib with larger needles.

Finishing

Weave in yarn ends. Block and allow to dry completely
before wearing.

Tips

- Let *Fixation* stretch as it wants when working it.

- Change colors by picking up new color from under
  previously used color. Do not cut.

✹ *From the Designer* ✹

"*Massachusetts is all about the weather. We love
spring for the brief moment it lasts, enjoy summer while
complaining about the heat, and are famous for our
glorious fall, chased away too soon by winter. The socks
are worked in the beautiful reds, oranges, golds and
browns of a sugar maple leaf at the height of seasonal
color. The winter white chases the fall color in a slipped
stitch mosaic variation that provides a sense of motion.*"

—*Susan Todhunter*

❧ Snowy Pines ❧

*M*aine brings to mind summer camps by the lake, lobster bakes, sunburned noses and hammocks slung between huge trees. There's no question that the state is a popular haven from the summer heat. Hardier year-round residents cherish the long, snowy winters. If you love knitting thick socks and wearing them most of the year, move to Maine!

These lovely socks by Rachel Covey Brown celebrate the beauty of snow covering the pines. They knit up quickly, either to snug into your boots, or to keep your feet warm in front of an open fire.

Sock Type: Cuff down on double-pointed needles

Finished Sizes: Adult S (M, L): Foot circumference: 7 (8, 9)" (18 [10, 23]cm); leg length to ankle: 7½" (19cm); foot length: 9 (9½, 10½)" (23 [24, 26.5]cm) (unstretched)

Project Gauge: 20 stitches and 26 rounds = 4" (10 cm) in stockinette stitch; 19 stitches and 22 rounds = 4" in stranded stockinette

Shopping List

Berroco *Vintage* (50% acrylic, 40% wool, 10% nylon, 217 yards/200m); 1 skein Douglas Fir #5177 (MC), 1 skein Snowy Day #5100 (CC)
Size US 6 (4.0mm) double-pointed needles
Stitch marker
Tapestry needle

Instructions

Cuff and leg
With MC, loosely CO 36 (40, 44) stitches. Ribbing round: *K2, p2; repeat from * to end. Continue ribbing as set for 1" (2.5cm). Work 1 round stockinette in MC. Join CC and work chart for selected size until chart is complete.

Heel
Cut MC. Heel is worked in CC.
Row 1 (RS): K17 (19, 21), w&t.
Row 2 (WS): P16 (18, 20), w&t.

Row 3: Knit to 1 stitch before previously wrapped stitch, w&t.

Row 4: Purl to 1 stitch before previously wrapped stitch, w&t.

Continue as set until four stitches remain unwrapped in the middle of the heel. Complete the short rows as follows:

Row 1: Knit to first wrapped stitch, work wrapped stitch together with its wrap, w&t.

Row 2: Purl to first wrapped stitch, work wrapped stitch together with its wrap, w&t.

Row 3: Knit to first double wrapped stitch, knit wrapped stitch together with both its wraps, w&t.

Row 4: Purl to first double wrapped stitch, purl wrapped stitch together with both its wraps, w&t.

Repeat rows 3-4 until all 18 (20, 22) heel stitches have been worked, ending with a WS row. Cut CC and reattach MC.

Foot

Work foot in the round in stockinette with MC until foot measures 7 (7½ , 8½)" [18 (19, 22)cm] long or approximately 2" (5cm) less then desired length. Cut MC and reattach CC.

Toe

Round 1 and all odd numbered rounds: Knit all stitches.

Round 2: *K7 (8, 9), k2tog; repeat from * to end.

Round 4: *K6 (7, 8), k2tog; repeat from * to end.

Round 6: *K5 (6, 7), k2tog; repeat from * to end.

Round 8: *K4 (5, 6), k2tog; repeat from * to end.

Round 10: *K3 (4, 5), k2tog; repeat from * to end.

Round 12: *K2 (3, 4), k2tog; repeat from * to end.

Round 14: *K1 (2, 3), k2tog; repeat from * to end.

Round 16 (M and L only): *K1 (2), k2tog; repeat from * to end.

Round 18 (L only): *K1, k2tog; repeat from * to end.

Cut CC, leaving a 6" (15cm) tail. Thread tail through the remaining eight stitches and pull tight.

Finishing

Weave in all ends. Block.

Tips

- Where you carry the non-working color over more than three or four stitches, make sure to weave in your floats. Stagger the weaving-in on consecutive rounds to help prevent gaps or floats showing through over these longer color sections.

✤ *From the Designer* ✤

"*I grew up in Boston, but spent much of my vacation time in Maine at my grandparents' house on the coast, or tucked away in the family cabin in the northern woods watching the snow come down and dreaming about skiing the next day. In both places, the landscape is dominated by pine trees of every sort — hemlocks, junipers, red pine, white pine — filling the air with the indescribable scent of fresh pine.*"

— Rachel Covey Brown

Small

Medium

Large

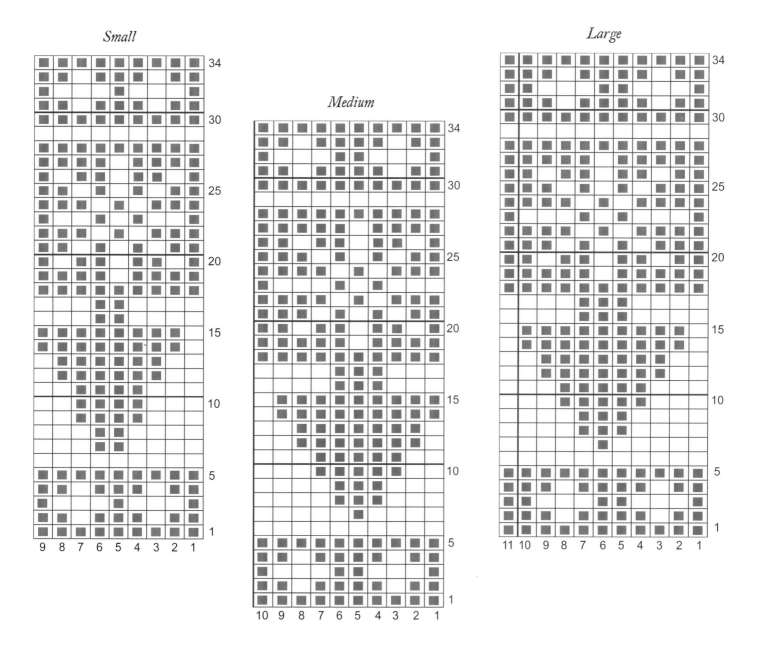

❧ Jersey Turnpike ❧

If you're headed north or south in New Jersey, there's no avoiding the dreaded Jersey Turnpike. One of the most traveled and dangerous roadways in the country, it can be confusing to Turnpike newbies and veterans alike. With anywhere from 4 to 14 lanes, it gets even more challenging when the lanes change direction from north to south and south to north at different times during the day.

These socks, by Heatherly Walker, are inspired by the challenge of navigating the Turnpike. The color is a nod to the 122 miles of asphalt and stripes. Start your needles!

Sock Type: Cuff down

Finished Size: Adult M (L): Foot circumference 7½ (8¼)" (19 [21]cm); leg length to ankle 6" (15cm); foot length 9" (23cm) or to fit (unstretched)

Project Gauge: 36 stitches and 44 rounds = 4" (10cm) in stockinette stitch; 38 stitches and 38 rounds = 4" (10cm) in stranded stockinette

Shopping List
Cascade Yarns *Heritage Sock* (75% superwash wool, 25% nylon, 437 yards/400m); 1 skein Snow #5618 (MC), 1 skein Real Black #5672 (CC)
Size US 2 (2.75 mm) needles
Tapestry needle

Stitch Guide
Corrugated Ribbing
*K2 (MC), p2 (CC); repeat from * to end. Note: Both yarns stay at back; move CC yarn to front to purl, and them move it to the back before you work the MC stitches.

Instructions
Cuff
With CC, CO 72 (80) stitches loosely, join to work in the round. Work *Corrugated Ribbing* for 1" (2.5cm).

Leg
Knit one round with CC only. Work Chart A twice around. Work as set until the chart is complete, then work rounds 1-16 again.

Heel
Break the MC yarn leaving 8" (20cm) tail and work heel back and forth on the next 36 (40) stitches with CC only. Knit the first heel row to last heel stitch, w&t. Slip the first stitch pwise, and then purl to the last stitch, w&t.
Sll pwise, knit across to the stitch before wrapped stitch, w&t. Continue knitting heel as established until 10 unwrapped stitches remain. The last wrapped stitch is on the WS. Turn and knit across to the first wrapped stitch, pick up wrap pwise and knit it together with stitch. Wrap the next stitch.
Work back and forth, picking up one stitch on each short row. Stop with last slipped stitch of heel on each side, wrap the stitch from instep to prevent holes at the corners of the heel. Pick up the wraps when you knit the first round.
Work Chart A beginning with round 17 across instep, and work Chart B across sole.
Continue as set until Chart A is complete, then work rounds 1-32 again. Foot should be 2" (5cm) short of desired length.

If more rounds are required, work from round 1 of chart again until desired length.

Toe
Arrange the sole stitches on one needle and foot stitches on the other. Using CC, work toe as follows:
Round 1: Knit.
Round 2 (decrease round): K1, ssk, k to last 3 stitches of instep, k2tog, k2, ssk, knit to last 3 stitches of round, k2tog, k1.
Repeat these 2 rounds four times, then repeat round 2 until 8 (12) stitches remain on each needle. Break yarn, leaving an 8" (20cm) tail.

Finishing
Graft toe closed using Kitchener Stitch. (See page 91). Weave in ends.

Tips
 ❖ If you have high arches, to add depth to the heel, knit first row plainly, work 4 short rows, then knit one plain row- picking up wraps, before beginning short rows for heel.

✦ *From the Designer* ✦

"Living on the East Coast most of my childhood, we would hear the grown ups talk about the Garden State and the ominous New Jersey Turnpike. By the time we hit the state border, we kids were always asleep. It wasn't until I was grown and driving on my own that I realized why the adults had spent so much time discussing which route to take. It was more magical when we were children."

— *Heatherly Walker*

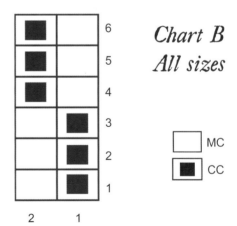

Chart B
All sizes

☐ MC
■ CC

Chart A – Medium

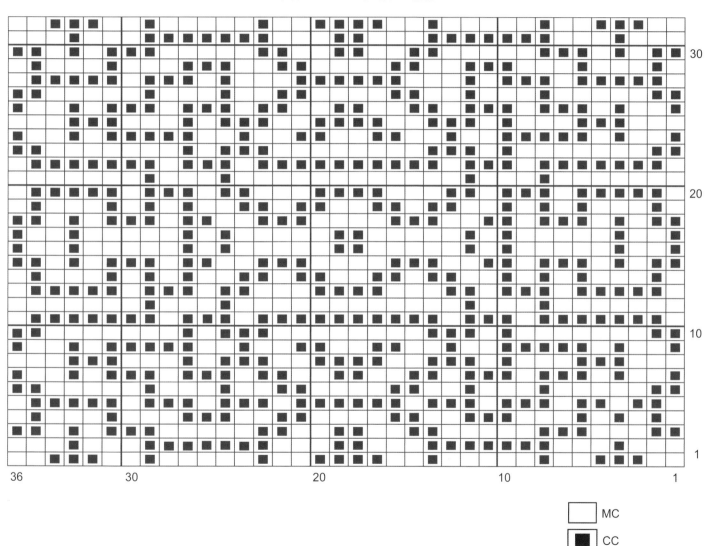

MC
CC

Chart A - Large

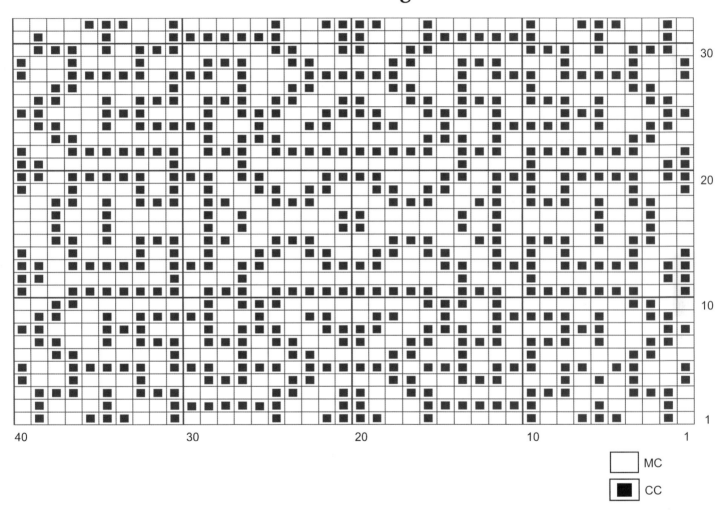

MC

CC

The Shot Heard Around the World

Many of the American Revolution's most popular historic sites are located in the Northeast. New York, New Jersey, Pennsylvania and Massachusetts are especially rich in preserved historical sites marking our country's founding.

Washington's Headquarters at Valley Forge, Pennsylvania and the Valley Forge National Historical Park are tributes to the extraordinary hardships endured by our Colonial patriots. In December, 1777, General George Washington moved his ragged, starving Continental Army troops to Valley Forge. The army erected 1,000 tents for its 12,000 soldiers and dug in for the winter. Washington, and later his wife as well, lived on the second floor of the house that served as Headquarters, with army business conducted on the ground floor. The park includes historical and recreated buildings, the Washington Memorial Chapel, built in 1903, and a carillon with bells representing each of the states and U.S. territories.

"One if by land, two if by sea" was the signal to be lit in the bell tower of Boston's Old North Church, as known to all American schoolchildren from Longfellow's poem "Paul Revere's Ride." On April 18, 1775, two lanterns shined from the tower, warning Charlestown patriots of the advance of British troops. Word was spread by riders to Lexington and Concord and from there to dozens more towns and villages. The historic church, open year-round for tours, includes lovely gardens planted with 18th century annuals and perennials.

You can find information on these and hundreds of other Revolutionary War sites by visiting the National Park Service website at www.nps.gov.

ᕦ Appalachian Trail ᕤ

The Appalachian Trail is the holy grail for American hikers. As it winds its way along the Appalachian mountain range from Georgia to Maine, intrepid hikers are rewarded with mountain, pasture and forest views along its 2,184 miles. Started in 1921 and built completely by private citizens, the trail is managed by the U.S. Park Service but maintained by thousands of volunteers.

Kimberly de la Cruz designed these socks with a winding trail of leafy twists and a lush, fresh color to pay tribute to the Pennsylvania section of the AT. They are too pretty to hide in hiking boots, though.

Sock Type: Cuff down, magic loop

Finished Size: Adult Medium: Foot circumference 7" (18cm); leg length to ankle 5½" (14cm); foot length 8" (20]cm) (unstretched)

Project Gauge: 36 stitches and 50 rounds = 4" (10cm) in stockinette stitch; 45 stitches and 46 rounds = 4" (10cm) in *Winding Trail Pattern*

Shopping List
Lorna's Laces *Shepherd Sock* (80% Superwash Merino; 20% Nylon, 435 yards/398m); 1 skein Catalpa #310
Size US 1 (2.25mm) 32" (80mm) circular needle.
Stitch markers
Tapestry needle

Abbreviations
Left Twist (LT):
Skip first stitch, knit in back of second stitch on left-hand needle, knit in first stitch and slip both stitches to right hand needle.

Right Twist (RT):
Skip first stitch, knit in front of second stitch on left-hand needle, knit in first stitch and slip both stitches to right hand needle.

Stitch Guide
Winding Trail Pattern
Round 1: P3, k2tog, yo, p1, LT, p1, yo, ssk, p3.
Round 2: P3, k2, p1, k2, p1, k2, p3.

Round 3: P2, k2tog, yo, p1, RT, LT, p1, yo, ssk, p2.
Round 4: P2, k2, p1, k1, p2, k1, p1, k2, p2.
Round 5: P1, k2tog, yo, p1, RT, p2, LT, p1, yo, ssk, p1.
Round 6: (P1, k2) twice, k2, p2, (k2, p1) twice.
Round 7: P1, k2tog, yo, p1, k2, p2, k2, p1, yo, ssk, p1.
Round 8: Same as round 6.
Round 9: Same as round 5.
Round 10: Same as round 6.
Round 11: Same as round 7.
Round 12: Same as round 6.
Round 13: Same as round 5.
Round 14: Same as round 6.
Repeat these 14 rounds for pattern.

Instructions

Using circular needle, loosely CO 68 stitches. Arrange the stitches so you have 34 on each end of the needle. Join to work in the round, being careful not to twist, and place a marker to indicate the beginning of round.

Cuff
Work a 2x2 rib for 1" (2.5cm), or longer if you prefer.

Leg
Begin by knitting the first 10 stitches in stockinette stitch. Place a different colored marker than the beginning of round marker if you like, to help keep track of where the chart begins. Refer to *Winding Trail Pattern* chart, or written instructions for the pattern, and begin working round 1 (14 stitches). Place another marker if needed to mark the end of the chart. Continue working in stockinette stitch until you have reached the end of the round. Continue in this manner until all 14 rounds of the chart have been worked a total of three times. Work another full repeat, and on the final round, work halfway across the round (stop after the 34 stitches of the first needle) and do not complete the round.

Heel Flap
Note: The heel flap is worked across the last 34 stitches of the round.
Row 1 (RS): *Sl1, k1, repeat from * to end of heel flap (34 stitches). Turn.

Row 2 (WS): Sl1, purl across.
Repeat these 2 rows seventeen more times, then row 1 once more, ending with WS facing (36 rows total).

Turning the heel
Row 1 (WS): Sl1, p19, p2tog, p1, turn.
Row 2 (RS): Sl1, k7, ssk, k1, turn.
Row 3: Sl1, purl to 1 stitch before the gap, p2tog, p1, turn.
Row 4: Sl1, knit to 1 stitch before the gap, ssk, k1, turn.
Repeat rows 3-4 until all stitches have been worked. Do not turn after last row. The last 2 rows will end with p2tog and ssk, respectively. 20 stitches remain.

Gusset
Pick up and knit one stitch in each of 18 slipped stitches along side of heel flap. To work the 34 stitches on the top of the foot, k10, work the *Winding Trail Pattern* chart, k10. Pick up and knit 18 stitches along the other side of the heel flap. This position is new beginning of round; place marker.

Winding Trail Pattern

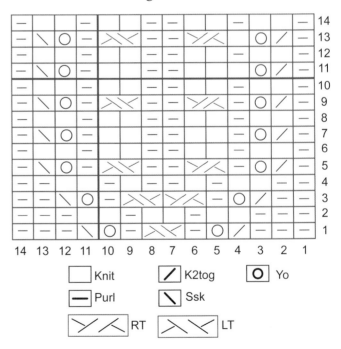

Knit | / K2tog | O Yo
— Purl | \ Ssk

⅄╱ RT ╱⅄ LT

Gusset decreases and foot
Round 1: Knit to 3 stitches before the end of Needle 2,
k2tog, k1. K10, work *Winding Trail Pattern* chart, k10 on
Needle 1. K1, ssk, knit to end of round on Needle 2.
Round 2: Knit remaining stitches on Needle 2, k10, work
chart, k10 on Needle 1, knit to beginning of round marker
on Needle 2.
Repeat these 2 rounds until 68 stitches remain (34 on each
needle).
Continue working foot without shaping, repeating round
2 only, until the foot measures 8" (20cm), or 2" (5cm) less
than total desired length, ending with an even-numbered
round on the chart. Remove beginning of round marker
during last round and place it at beginning of Needle 1.

Toe Decreases
Round 1: Knit all stitches on both needles.
Round 2: Needle 1: k1, ssk, knit to last 3 stitches, k2tog, k1.
Repeat for Needle 2.
Repeat these 2 rounds until 8 stitches remain on each
needle (16 stitches total).

Finishing
Graft toe closed using Kitchener Stitch. (See page 91).
Weave in ends.

✦ *From the Designer* ✦

"*My design is inspired by Pennsylvania and the famous
Appalachian Trail that passes through the eastern
corner of the state on its way from Maryland to New
Jersey. The design represents the peaks of the mountains
and the twists and turns of the trail that winds its way
through the area.*"

— *Kimberly de la Cruz*

Cranberry Nut Fudge

I love Cape Cod, especially Martha's Vineyard and Nantucket. I also love cranberries. All of this comes together in a classic seaside resort treat I first tasted in Hyannis Port and looked forward to on every visit. Fudge shops are everywhere on the Northeast coast. Along the Cape, cranberry fudge puts a local twist on an all-American candy. The berries cut the sweetness of the fudge with a wonderful burst of tartness. I like adding pistachios rather than walnuts when I make this for the holidays.

Directions

Line bottom and sides of an 8x8" pan with foil or wax paper. Butter the lining with 1 tsp of butter and set pan aside. In a medium saucepan over medium heat, bring sugar, sour cream and remaining ½ c. butter to a boil. Boil, stirring, until candy thermometer reaches 234° or soft ball stage. Remove from heat and immediately add white chocolate chips, marshmallow creme and vanilla. Beat with a wooden spoon until smooth. Fold in the dried cranberries and nuts. Quickly pour the mixture into the prepared pan and allow to cool at room temperature.

Use the pan lining to lift fudge out of pan. Peel off the lining. Using a very sharp knife dipped in hot water, cut into 1" squares. Dip and dry knife between cuts. Store in airtight container in the refrigerator. Best if consumed within 1 week, but it's unlikely it will last that long.

Makes 64 squares, about 3 lbs in weight.

Shopping List

1 tsp plus ½ c. butter, divided

2 c. sugar

¾ c. sour cream

1 package (10-12 oz) white chocolate chips

1 jar (7 oz.) marshmallow creme

1 tsp vanilla extract

1 c. pistachios or walnuts, coarsely chopped

1 c. dried cranberries, coarsely chopped

South Carolina

Southeast

The Southeast has been home for most of my life; I grew up in Florida and still live there most of the year. The rest of the year, I live in the mountains of North Carolina, and I've lived in Georgia and Mississippi as well. Even without fried pickle chips and red velvet cake, the region's beautiful beaches and the Blue Ridge Mountains would have convinced me to choose the Southeast as my home.

No part of the country likely has such a wide range of climates and nature. The land once known as "Dixie" has something for everyone: tropical bougainvillea and royal palms in South Florida, wild barrier islands off the Georgia coast, beautiful beaches on the Gulf of Mexico, and the mighty Appalachian Mountain range, stretching from Georgia up through West Virginia. Intrepid adventurers could spend the morning surfing the East Coast's largest waves at Cocoa Beach, Florida and sleep under clear, starry mountain skies that night at Beech Mountain, North Carolina, the highest town east of the Rockies.

In addition to its myriad natural wonders, the history of the country starts here, in the nation's oldest city, St. Augustine, Florida. The Southeastern states are home to some of the most significant historical sites from both the Revolutionary and Civil Wars. For a painless educational trip with the family, you can't beat Colonial Williamsburg for a lesson on 18th century American life and the politics leading to independence. For travelers with an interest in more recent history, walk in the steps of the first space explorers at Cape Canaveral and the Kennedy Space Center.

If nature and history aren't your thing, you can always eat your way across the Southeast. Maybe I'm prejudiced, but I think this is where you'll find the tastiest regional food in the country. Where else have cooks perfected the art of frying almost anything? From pickles and asparagus, for appetizers, steak and chicken for your main dish and pies for dessert, everything tastes better fried. Schedule a bit of hiking so you can get home without having to shop for bigger pants.

Alpine Meadow Bed Socks

For four months each year, I live in the Blue Ridge Mountains of North Carolina. After decades of living in Florida where the summer means brown grass and dead blooms, it was a revelation to see the glory of an Alpine summer right outside my door. I was entranced by the flowers and the beautiful Eastern Tiger Swallowtail butterflies that landed on my deck and danced among the trees — magic.

These cozy bed socks, with a butterfly stitch and floral embroidery, are a perfect bit of summer's beauty for your feet on chilly winter mornings.

Sock Type: Toe up on two circular needles

Finished Size: Adult Medium: Foot circumference 9" (23cm); leg length from ankle 3½" (9cm) including picot; foot length 9" (23cm) (unstretched)

Project Gauge: 21 stitches and 30 rounds = 4" (10cm) in stockinette stitch; 18½ stitches and 35 rounds = 4" (10cm) in *Butterfly Stitch Pattern*

Shopping List

Classic Elite *Liberty Wool* (100% superwash wool, 122 yards/112m); 2 skeins Ecru #7816
Small amounts of sportweight superwash for flowers, leaves and centers. Shown in Cascade Yarns *220 Superwash Sport* in Pink Ice #836, Periwinkle #844, Strawberry Cream #894, Daffodil #821, Lemon #820, and Green Apple #802
US Size 6 (4mm) circular needles (2 sets)
US Size 6 (4mm) double-pointed needles or stitch holders
Tapestry needle

Stitch Guide

Butterfly Stitch Pattern (worked over multiples of 14 plus 11)
Round 1: K2, wyif sl7, move yarn to back, k7, with wyif sl7, move yarn to back, k2.
Round 2: Knit.
Round 3: Same as round 1.
Rounds 4-5: Knit.

Round 6: Same as round 1.
Round 7: Knit.
Round 8: Same as round 1.
Round 9: Knit.
Round 10: Same as round 1.
Round 11: K5, insert RH needle from top to bottom under loose strands and lift onto LH needle, knit next live stitch together with the lifted strands, k13, insert RH needle from top to bottom under loose strands and lift onto LH needle, knit next live stitch together with the lifted strands, k5.
Round 12: Knit.
Round 13: K9, wyif slip 7, move yarn to back, k9.
Round 14: Knit.
Round 15: Same as round 13.
Rounds 16-17: Knit.
Round 18: Same as round 13.
Round 19: Knit.
Round 20: Same as round 13.
Round 21: Knit.
Round 22: Same as round 13.
Round 23: K12, insert RH needle from top to bottom under loose strands and lift onto LH needle, knit next live stitch together with the lifted strands, k12.
Round 24: Knit.

Instructions

With Turkish Cast On or Judy's Magic Cast On, CO 20 stitches (10 on each needle).
Round 1: *K1f&b, knit to last stitch on needle, k1f&b; repeat from * to end.
Round 2: Knit.
Repeat these 2 rounds until there are 22 stitches on each needle, ending with a round 2.
Needle 1 holds instep stitches; Needle 2 holds sole stitches.

Foot
Round 1: Needle 1: k1f&b, knit half way across, m1, knit to last stitch, k1f&b (25 stitches); Needle 2: knit (22 stitches). Work *Butterfly Stitch Pattern* across next 25 stitches, knit to end of round. Work as set for 1½ repeats of *Butterfly Stitch Pattern* or until sock reaches the point where the top of the foot meets the front of the leg without stretching.

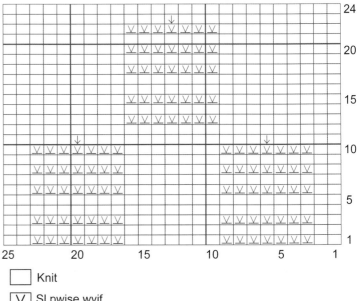

Butterfly Stitch Chart
25 instep stitches shown

☐ Knit

Ⓥ Sl pwise wyif

↓ Insert RH needle from top to bottom behind loose strands, lift onto LH needle and knit together with next stitch

Gusset
Keeping Needle 1 in *Butterfly Stitch Pattern*, work gusset increases on Needle 2 as follows:
Round 1: Needle 1 in pattern; Needle 2: k1, m1, knit to last stitch, m1, k1.
Round 2: Needle 1 in pattern; Needle 2: knit.
Repeat these 2 rounds five more times (25 stitches on Needle 1; 34 stitches on Needle 2).

Heel Extension
Work across Needle 1 in pattern. Knit the first 11 stitches of Needle 2 onto a double-pointed needle or stitch holder. Working Needle 2, ssk, knit the next 10 stitches. These 11 stitches will be worked back and forth for the heel extension. Hold remaining 11 remaining gusset stitches. Working the 11 stitches remaining on Needle 2, turn, p2tog, purl to the end. Turn, ssk, knit to end. Continue working

in stockinette, decreasing as set in these 2 rows, until 4 stitches remain and ending with a **WS** row. Pick up and purl 8 stitches along the decrease edge. Turn and knit across all 12 stitches and then pick up and knit 8 stitches along the remaining decrease edge. Turn and purl back across the 20 heel stitches.

Heel Flap
Work heel flap upward, working back and forth, incorporating one stitch from the adjacent double-pointed needle or stitch holder at the beginning of each row with a k2tog through the back loop or p2tog through the back loop. Work until all held stitches are incorporated and ending with a WS row.

Leg
Knit across heel stitches, increasing one stitch at the center of the heel. Knit the first stitch from Needle 1 onto Needle 2 (23 stitches on Needle 2). Work the next round of *Butterfly Stitch* Pattern on Needle 1, starting with stitch 2 of the chart/instructions (stitch 1 is now on Needle 2), to the last stitch. Knit the last stitch of Needle 1 onto Needle 2 (23 stitches on each needle). On Needle 2, work in stockinette until Needle 1 is being worked with either round 1 or round 13 of the chart, leaving off the first and last stitch of the pattern for both repeats. Then begin working both needles

in *Butterfly Stitch*, working Needle 2 so that when round 1 is worked on Needle 1, round 14 is worked on Needle 2. Continue working in pattern for a full 24 round repeat on the back of the leg or until desired length, ending with a round 12 or 24. Work even in stockinette for 2 rounds.

Cuff
Work 4 rounds of 1x1 rib. BO using *Picot Chain Bind Off* as follows (even number of stitches):
BO 2 stitches, * move remaining stitch on RH needle to LH needle, using cable cast on method, CO 3 stitches, BO 5 stitches; repeat from * to end. Fasten off last stitch.

Finishing
Embroider flowers and leaves onto sock using photos/chart as a guide. Flowers and leaves shown are worked in Satin Stitch, centers in Spider Stitch. Weave in all ends.

Tips
- ❖ You can embroider the instep before you turn the heel or embroider when done, slipping cardboard into the sock to prevent stitching through the sock.

- ❖ You can find videos for all the embroidery stitches at PurlQueenPatterns.com and on PlanetPurl.com.

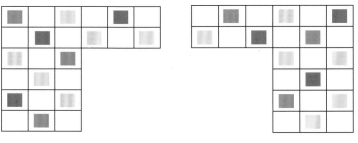

Sock 1   Sock 2

Satin Stitch

Come up from back at base of first stitch, leaving 6" (15cm) tail.

Go in from front to back to make desired length of stitch. Come up from back next to the base of the first stitch.

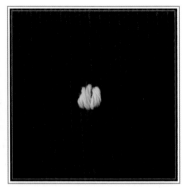

Continue placing stitches of desired length next to each other. Finish through back. Weave in ends.

Spider Web Stitch

Come up from back at the center of the spider web, leaving 6" (15cm) tail.

Make seven evenly spaced spokes, always coming up through same center spot.

Weave over and under each spoke, keeping the yarn circles close together and flat.

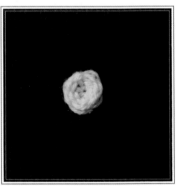

Continue weaving until spokes are full. Go through back. Weave in ends.

Spring in the High Country

One beautiful late spring day, when I was hiking with my dogs in North Carolina, I came upon a National Park Service truck parked high up along the side of the trail. The ranger was making a butterfly survey — a very cool job! I asked him about the gorgeous butterflies that were everywhere, flitting around at outdoor cafés, decorating fields of flowers, and keeping me company in my garden. "Eastern Swallowtails," he informed me. Beautiful iridescent blues and vivid oranges and yellows dancing on the breeze. Lovely.

For most of the Southeast, spring temperatures are already so high that blooms are on the wane. But the mountains? They are exploding into a magnificent show of alpine flora. The Blue Ridge Parkway in April and May is a sea of Catawba and Carolina rhododendrons in full bloom. A little later, the mountainsides are carpeted with buttercups, trillium, bluets, wild geranium, columbine, and Queen Anne's Lace — a favorite of the butterflies.

April and May are the best months to visit the legendary gardens at the Biltmore Estate. The Spring Flower Festival features more than 100,000 tulips and other spring bulbs, plus poppies, pansies, snapdragons and a plethora of annuals throughout the property. The natural gardens are awash with acre after acre of blooming rhododendrons in pink, red and white. Visit on a sunny day and plan to spend at least half your time wandering. It's spring in the Carolina High Country, dressed in its finest.

꙰ Land & Sea ꙰

Florida is rightfully famous for its white sand beaches. With 1200 miles of coastline, Florida has half again as much beach as California. From the "Redneck Riviera" in the panhandle, the swanky beaches of Naples and the Treasure Coast, the tropical colors of Key West, the star-studded waterfront bistros of South Beach, to the unspoiled wild dunes of Amelia Island, you're sure to find your perfect spot of sand.

Designer Emily Marshall found her ideal beach and celebrates it with these beautiful socks, inspired by the waves and dunes of Florida's defining feature. Slip them on and feel the salt breeze on your face.

Sock Type: Toe up with magic loop method

Finished Size: Adult Medium: Foot circumference 7" (18cm); leg length from ankle 7" (18cm); foot length 9" (23cm) or to fit (unstretched)

Project Gauge: 36 stitches and 44 rounds = 4" (10cm) in stockinette stitch; 38 stitches and 44 rounds = 4" (10cm) in *Waves Pattern*

Shopping List
Crystal Palace Yarn *Panda Silk* (52% bamboo, 43% superwash merino wool, 5% combed silk, 204 yards/188m); 2 skeins Butterscotch #3002
Size US 2 (2.75mm) 32" (80cm) or 40" (100cm) circular needle
Stitch markers
Tapestry needle

Stitch Guide
Climbing Leaves Pattern
Round 1 (set-up round): P8, k3, p4, k5, p4.
Round 2: P6, p2tog, k1, m1 pwise, k2, p4, k2, yo, k1, yo, k2, p4.
Round 3: P7, k1, p1, k2, p4, k7, p4.
Round 4: P5, p2tog, k1, m1 pwise, p1, k2, p4, k3, yo, k1, yo, k3, p4.
Round 5: P6, k1, p2, k2, p4, k9, p4.
Round 6: P4, p2tog, k1, p1, m1 pwise, p1, k2, p4, ssk, k5, k2tog, p4.
Round 7: P5, k1, p3, k2, p4, k7, p4.

Round 8: P3, p2tog, k1, p2, m1 pwise, p1, k2, p4, ssk, k3, k2tog, p4.
Round 9: P4, k1, p4, k2, p4, k5, p4.
Round 10: P4, yo, k1, yo, p4, k2, p4, ssk, k1, k2tog, p4.
Round 11: P4, k3, p4, k2, p4, k3, p4.
Round 12: P4, yo, k1, yo, k2, p4, k1, yo, k1, p2tog, p2, sk2p, p4.
Round 13: P4, k5, p4, k3, p8.
Round 14: P4, k2, yo, k1, yo, k2, p4, k2, m1 pwise, k1, p2tog, p6.
Round 15: P4, k7, p4, k2, p1, k1, p7.
Round 16: P4, k3, yo, k1, yo, k3, p4, k2, p1, m1 pwise, k1, p2tog, p5.
Round 17: P4, k9, p4, k2, p2, k1, p6.
Round 18: P4, ssk, k5, k2tog, p4, k2, p1, m1 pwise, p1, k1, p2tog, p4.
Round 19: P4, k7, p4, k2, p3, k1, p5.
Round 20: P4, ssk, k3, k2tog, p4, k2, p1, m1 pwise, p2, k1, p2tog, p3.
Round 21: P4, k5, p4, k2, p4, k1, p4.
Round 22: P4, ssk, k1, k2tog, p4, k2, p4, yo, k1, yo, p4.
Round 23: P4, k3, p4, k2, p4, k3, p4.
Round 24: P4, sk2p, p2, p2tog, k1, yo, k1, p4, yo, k1, yo, k2, p4.
Round 25: P8, k3, p4, k5, p4.
Repeat rounds 2-25 for pattern.

Waves Pattern
Round 1: Knit.
Round 2: *K2tog twice, (yo, k1) four times, k2tog twice; repeat from * to end.
Rounds 3-4: Knit.

Instructions
Using Judy's Magic Cast On, CO 16 stitches (8 instep stitches and 8 sole stitches).

Toe
Pm to mark beginning of round.
Round 1: Knit.
Round 2: K1f&b, knit to 2 stitches before end, k1f&b, k1.
Repeat for sole stitches.

Repeat these 2 rounds, increasing 4 stitches on every other row, until you have 64 stitches total.

Foot
Instep: K4, pm, work round 1 of *Waves Pattern*, pm, k4. Work in stockinette stitch on the sole stitches. Continue as established until the foot measures 1¾" (4cm) short of desired length.

Heel Cup
Row 1: K31, w&t.
Row 2: P30, w&t.
Row 3: Knit to 1 stitch before last wrapped stitch, w&t.
Row 4: Purl to 1 stitch before last wrapped stitch, w&t.
Repeat rows 3-4 eight more times (10 wrapped stitches, 12 unwrapped stitches, 10 wrapped stitches).

Heel Flap
Row 1: Knit to first wrapped stitch, knit the wrap and stitch together, turn.
Row 2: Sl1, purl to first wrapped stitch, purl wrap and stitch together, turn.
Row 3: Sl1, knit to next wrapped stitch, knit the wrap and stitch together, turn.
Row 4: Sl1, purl to next wrapped stitch, purl the wrap and stitch together, turn.
Repeat rows 3-4 seven times.(1 wrapped stitch each side).
Next round: Sl1, knit to last wrapped stitch, knit wrap and

✻ *From the Designer* ✻

"When I think of Florida, I see its two sides: the beach with waves and sand, and its trees and lush plant life. I wanted to pay homage to both sides so I created a pattern that displayed characteristics of each. I used a sand-colored yarn of bamboo, wool and silk to keep the socks lightweight."

— Emily Marshall

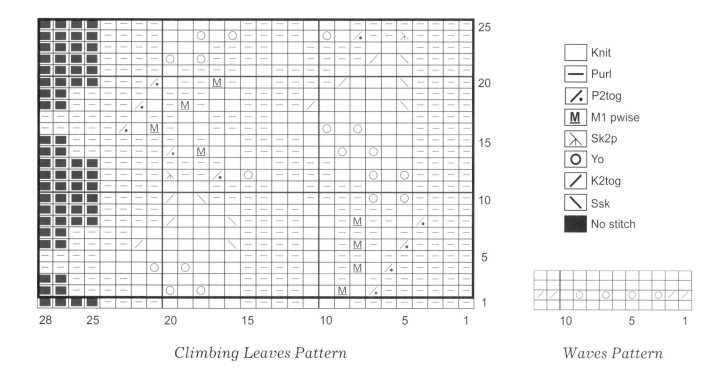

Knit
— Purl
⟋• P2tog
M M1 pwise
⅄ Sk2p
O Yo
⟋ K2tog
⟍ Ssk
■ No stitch

Climbing Leaves Pattern

Waves Pattern

stitch together. Next work the instep stitches in pattern and knit the wrap and stitch together, then knit across.

Leg
Knit instep stitches in *Waves Pattern* established. On sole stitches: K4, pm, work set-up round of *Climbing Leaves Pattern*, pm, knit to end. Continue in pattern, working *Waves Pattern* on instep stitches and *Climbing Leaves Pattern* on sole stitches. Work 3 repeats of *Climbing Leaves Pattern* then begin the cuff.

Cuff
*K2, p2; repeat from * to end. Continue in 2x2 ribbing for as set at least 1½" (4cm). BO in your favorite stretchy bind off.

Finishing
Weave in ends. Block if desired.

Tips
- In order to make working the 2 lace patterns at once easier, start the *Climbing Leaves Pattern* on a row 1 repeat of the *Waves Pattern*. Then the patterned row of the *Waves Pattern* is on rows 2, 6, 10, 14, 18 and 22.

- Pick up a stitch between the last wrap and the first instep stitch, knitting them together. It helps stop any holes showing in the heel. Repeat this for the other side as well.

❧ Nana's Garden ☙

Kentucky is far enough north to (usually) avoid the scorching heat of the states farther south, but still "southern" enough to allow for a long and bountiful growing season. The result? Gardeners' heaven. In addition to beautiful public gardens and arboretums, many Kentuckian's create thriving patches of blooms and vegetables in their own backyards.

Designer Lynn Taylor found inspiration in her friend Nana's garden. Nana is a knitter as well as a master gardener. The delicate lacy cabled rib and fresh color celebrate the result of Nana's hard work.

Sock Type: Cuff down on double-pointed needles

Finished Size: Adult Medium: Foot circumference 6½" (16.5cm); leg length to ankle 7" (18cm); foot length 9½" (24cm) (unstretched)

Project Gauge: 32 stitches and 42 rounds = 4" (10cm) in stockinette stitch; 44 stitches and 44 rounds = 4" (10cm) in *Lacy Fern Rib Pattern* (unstretched)

Shopping List
Alpaca with a Twist *Socrates* (30% baby alpaca, 30% merino wool, 20% bamboo, 20% nylon, 400 yards/188m); 1 skein Wednesday Night Green #4018
Size US 2 (2.75mm) double-pointed needles
Stitch marker
Tapestry needle

Abbreviations
RT (Right Twist)
K2tog but leave stitches on needle. Knit the first stitch again and slip both stitches off needle.

Stitch Guide
Lacy Fern Rib Pattern
Round 1: *Ssk, k1, yo, k1, yo, k1, k2tog, p2, k2, p2; repeat from * to end of round.
Rounds 2-3: *K7, p2, k2, p2; repeat from * to end.
Round 4: *K7, p2, RT, p2; repeat from * to end.
Repeat rounds 1-4 for pattern.

Instructions

CO 65 stitches. Divide stitches over 3 double-pointed needles as follows: Needle 1: 26 stitches; Needle 2: 13 stitches; and Needle 3: 26 stitches. Join to work in the round being careful not to twist. Place marker to mark beginning of the round.

Cuff

Rounds 1-3: *K3, p1, k3, p2, k2, p2; repeat from * to end of round.
Round 4: *K3, p1, k3, p2, RT, p2; repeat from * to end of round.
Repeat rounds 1-4 for 1½" (4cm), ending with round 3.

Leg

Work rounds 1-4 of *Lacy Fern Rib Pattern* fifteen times or until you reach your desired length, ending with round 4.

Heel flap

Note: Slip stitches pwise.
Set-up row: Work row 1 of pattern across the next 25 stitches. Slip remaining stitch to next needle; turn.
Sl1, p13, p1f&b, p15. You will be working back and forth in rows on these 31 stitches to form the heel flap.
Row 1: Sl1, RT, *k1, sl1; repeat from * to last 4 stitches, k1, LT, k1.
Row 2: Sl1, p30.
Repeat rows 1-2 until heel measures 2¼"-2½" (6-6.5cm), ending with row 2.

Heel turn

Row 1 (RS): Sl1, k17, ssk, k1, turn.
Row 2: Sl1, p6, p2tog, p1, turn.
Row 3: Sl1, knit to 1 stitch before gap, ssk, k1, turn.
Row 4: Sl1, purl to 1 stitch before gap, p2tog, p1, turn.
Repeat rows 3-4 until all stitches have been worked and 19 stitches remain.
Next row: Sl1, k2tog, k16. (18 stitches)

Gusset

Using same needle that the remaining heel stitches are on, pick up and knit 1 stitch in each slipped stitch along heel flap. With an empty needle, continue pattern as set across next 35 stitches. Note: The leg pattern now begins and ends with a purl stitch. With an empty needle, pick up and knit 1 stitch in each slipped stitch along heel flap and knit 9 stitches from heel onto this needle.
Round 1: Needle 1: knit to last 3 stitches, k2tog, k1; Needle 2: next leg pattern row; Needle 3: k1, ssk, knit to the end.
Round 2: Needle 1: knit; Needle 2: next leg pattern row; Needle 3: knit.
Work rounds 1-2 until you reach 15 stitches on Needles 1 and 3. Continue even in pattern as set until the foot reaches 1½" (4cm) less than your desired length.

Toe shaping

To even up heel stitches in preparation for the toe, slip the beginning purl stitch of Needle 2 to Needle 1 and the ending purl stitch of Needle 2 to Needle 3. Knit one round, knitting

Lacy Fern Rib Pattern

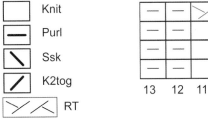

		Knit
—		Purl
\		Ssk
/		K2tog
⅄⋌		RT

2 stitches together in center of Needle 2. (64 stitches).

Round 1: Needle 1: knit to last 3 stitches., k2tog, kl; Needle 2: kl, ssk, knit to last 3 stitches, k2tog, kl; Needle 3: kl, ssk, knit to end.

Round 2: Knit across all 3 needles.

Repeat these 2 rounds until there are 8 stitches on Needles 1 and 3 and 16 stitches on Needle 2. Knit stitches from Needle 1 onto Needle 3. Decrease every round by repeating round 1 until there are 4 stitches on Needles 1 and 3 and 8 stitches on Needle 2.

Finishing

Graft toe closed using Kitchener Stitch. (See page 91). Weave in all ends. Block if desired.

✦ *From the Designer* ✦

"I designed this sock for my friend Leslie, known as 'Nana' to her family. The pathways of the sock remind me of life's path, sometimes smooth and sometimes full of twists and turns, just like Nana's beautiful garden."

— *Lynn Taylor*

Fried Apple Pies

Moses Cone Park, near Blowing Rock, North Carolina, is the perfect place to hike. The park boasts over 25 miles of carriage trails, winding through old orchards that once boasted 75 varieties of apples. Every autumn, the area's roadside vendors sell all things apple — apple butter, apple cider, caramel apples and my favorite, fried apple pies. Hot from the fryer and glistening with a sprinkle of cinnamon sugar, they are a true Carolina treat.

Directions

For filling: Melt butter over medium-low heat in large fry pan. Add apples and raisins and sauté until apples are soft. Add remaining filling ingredients and continue cooking until sugar is dissolved. Set aside to cool completely.

For pastry: Sift flour with salt into mixing bowl. Cut in butter. Add enough ice water to make a stiff dough. Divide dough in half and roll each half into a ball. Place in plastic bag or wrap with foil and put in refrigerator for 30 minutes. Working with half of the dough at a time, roll out to about ¼" thick. Cut 4-5" circles of pastry. Refrigerate first half while rolling out second half. Brush edges with cold water. Place 1-2 Tbl of filling in center of each circle. Fold in half using the tines of a fork to seal the edges. Prick one side with a fork to vent.

In a skillet, heat approximately 2 c. of oil to 300-350°. Carefully slide a few pies into the oil and brown on one side. Turn pie over (carefully!) and brown second side. Drain on paper towels for 5 minutes and then sprinkle with granulated sugar.

Serve warm.

Shopping List

Pastry
2 c. sifted flour
¼ tsp salt
½ c. unsalted butter
6 Tbl ice water

Filling
4 Tbl butter
4 large fall apples, cut in half-inch dice
¾ c. granulated sugar
¼ c. dark brown sugar
1½ Tbl lemon juice
2 Tbl golden raisins
1 tsp lemon zest
¼ tsp salt
¼ tsp ground cinnamon
⅛ tsp ground allspice

For frying
Vegetable oil
2 Tbl granulated sugar

Midwest Wheat Field

Midwest

The Midwestern states keep most of the rest of the country fed. The magnificent "amber waves of grain" are rightfully immortalized in the lyrics of "America the Beautiful." But if you're an East Coast or West Coaster, you might be surprised that there's more to the Midwest than farmland, open skies and miles of rolling fields.

Chicago, our third largest city, is one of my favorites. I was born there and my son attended college in the South Loop. While he was in school, I loved to visit for the shopping, the vibrant theater community, and one of the world's best museums, the Art Institute. Whether you visit the stores of the Magnificent Mile, take in a play at the famous Steppenwolf Theater, or watch one of their five professional sports teams, I'm sure you'll fall in love with Chicago, too.

If you're after shopping on the biggest scale possible, Bloomington, Minnesota is the site of the country's largest mall. The Mall of America includes more than 400 stores, 50 restaurants, and even a Nickelodeon theme park. It attracts more than 40 million visitors every year.

For a trip back a century in time, head to Mackinac Island, Michigan. Grand Victorian hotels and historic B&B's evoke the sense of a time when the pace of life was more leisurely and ladies with parasols on the arms of men in straw boaters strolled the island during the summer season.

If you love live music and entertainment, Branson, Missouri is your Midwest vacation destination. A more family-friendly Las Vegas, Branson boasts more than 50 live-event theaters and attracts music's biggest stars. There's also plenty of golf, three lakes, and the historic downtown to keep you occupied between shows.

Cleveland's Rock and Roll Hall of Fame is, by itself, a great reason to visit Cleveland. Its 150,000 square feet includes four theaters and seven floors of exhibits, including such artifacts as the guitar John Lennon played at the Beatles' famous 1965 performance at Shea Stadium and the guitar on which Pete Townsend composed "Pinball Wizard." No question about it — "Cleveland rocks!"

From the Fields to the Stars

Ohio is a strong agricultural state, helping feed the country. The state also gave birth to those who dared to dream beyond the bounds of the Earth. The Wright brothers and twenty-four astronauts were born in Ohio, including John Glenn and Neil Armstrong.

These socks by Joy Gerhardt celebrate the Ohioans who work the earth, and those who slip its bonds. The toes of the socks, with their tiny twisted cables, are inspired by waving wheat. The fields transition to a sky dotted with shooting stars.

Sock Type: Toe up

Finished Sizes: Adult M (L): Foot circumference 7¾ (9½)" (19.5 [24]cm); leg length from ankle 6¼" (16cm); foot length to fit (unstretched)

Project Gauge: 38 stitches and 50 rounds = 4" (10 cm) in stockinette stitch, 40 stitches and 50 rounds = 4" (10 cm) in *Waving Grain Pattern*

Shopping List
Spud & Chloe *Fine* (80% superwash wool, 20% silk, 248 yards/227m); 1 skein each Bumble Bee #7811 (Color A) and Snorkel #7809 (Color B)
Size US 1 (2.25mm) double-pointed needles (set of 5)
Stitch marker
Tapestry needle

Abbreviations
Dyo: Yarnover twice, and on the following row, drop the second loop

Stitch Guide
Cable 2 right (C2R)
Slip two stitches together kwise, as if to work a k2tog. Return stitches to the left needle, and knit the first through the back loop and the second through the front loop.

Cable 2 left (C2L)
Slip two stitches one by one kwise, as if to work a ssk. Bring the left needle through them both from right to left, and slip them back to the left needle. Knit the first stitch through the front loop and the second stitch through the back loop.

Waving Grain Pattern (over multiple of 8 stitches + 2)
Rounds 1-5: P2, *p3, k1tbl, p4; repeat from * to end.
Round 6: P2, *p2, k2tog, m1, p4; repeat from * to end.
Round 7: P2, *p2, k2tbl, p4; repeat from * to end.
Round 8: P2, *p1, C2R, C2L, p3; repeat from * to end.
Round 9: P2, *p1, k4tbl, p3; repeat from * to end.

Rounds 10-13: Repeat rounds 8-9 twice more.
Rounds 14-18: P2, *p6, k1tbl, p1; repeat from * to last 8 stitches, p8.
Round 19: P2, *p5, k2tog, m1, p1; repeat from * to last 8 stitches, p8.
Round 20: P2, *p5, k2tbl, p1; repeat from * to last 8 stitches, p8.
Round 21: P2, *p4, C2R, C2L; repeat from * to last 8 stitches, p8.
Round 22: P2, *p4, k4tbl; repeat from * to last 8 stitches, p8.
Rounds 23-26: Repeat rounds 21-22 twice.
Repeat these 26 rounds for pattern.

Waving Grain Pattern

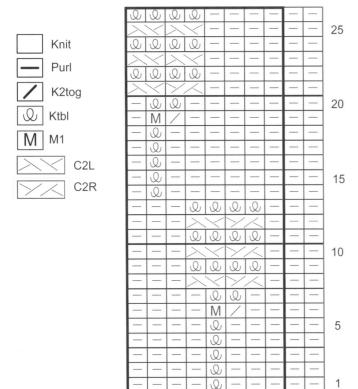

	Knit
—	Purl
/	K2tog
Ⓠ	Ktbl
M	M1
⤬	C2L
⤬	C2R

Shooting Stars Pattern

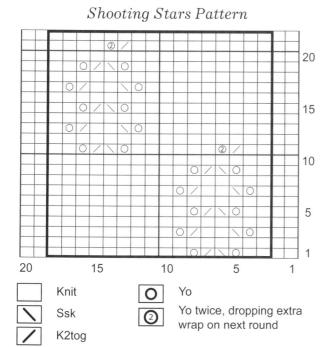

Knit			Yo
Ssk			Yo twice, dropping extra wrap on next round
K2tog			

Shooting Stars Pattern (over a multiple of 16 sts + 4)

Round 1: K2, *k2, yo, ssk, k2tog, yo, k10; repeat from * to last 2 stitches, k2.

Round 2 and all even-numbered rounds: Knit.

Round 3: K2, *k1, yo, ssk, k2, k2tog, yo, k9; repeat to last 2 stitches, k2.

Rounds 5 and 9: Same as round 1.

Round 7: Same as round 3.

Round 11: K2, *k2, k2tog, dyo, k6, yo, ssk, k2tog, yo, k2; repeat to last 2 stitches, k2.

Round 13: K2, *k9, yo, ssk, k2, k2tog, yo, k1; repeat from * to last 2 stitches, k2.

Round 15: K2, *k10, yo, ssk, k2tog, yo, k2; repeat from * to last 2 stitches, k2.

Round 17: Same as round 13.

Round 19: Same as round 15.

Round 21: K2, *k10, k2tog, dyo, k4; repeat from * to last 2 stitches, k2.

Round 22: Knit.

Instructions

Using Judy's Magic Cast On in Color A, CO 24 (32) stitches (12 [16] per needle). Distribute these stitches evenly to four double-pointed needles.

Round 1: Knit.

Round 2: (K2, m1, knit to last 2 stitches on needle, m1, k2) twice.

Work these two rounds until you have 68 (84) stitches total. Needles 1 and 2 are the instep, and needles 3 and 4 are the sole of the foot (always work sole stitches in stockinette).

Set-up round for Waving Grain Pattern: P2, *k3, k1tbl, k3, p1; repeat from * across instep.

Repeat the set-up round 6 times more.

For the remainder of the foot, work *Waving Grain Pattern* on instep and stockinette on sole. Continue in pattern as set until work measures 2" (5cm) less than total foot length, stopping at round 9 or 22.

Next round: Purl across instep, and place all 34 (42) sole stitches on one needle to begin short row heel.

Heel

Note: The heel is knit in short rows across the 34 (42) sole stitches.

Row 1: Knit to last heel stitch, w&t.

Row 2: Purl to last heel stitch, w&t.

Row 3: Knit to last unwrapped stitch, w&t.

Row 4: Purl to last unwrapped stitch, w&t.

Repeat rows 3-4 until there are 11 (14) wrapped stitches on either side, and 12 (14) unwrapped center heel stitches.

Next row (RS): Knit to first wrapped stitch, work wrapped stitch together with its wrap, w&t the following stitch.

Next row (WS): Purl to first wrapped stitch, work wrapped stitch together with its wrap, w&t the following stitch.

Next row: Knit to first wrapped stitch (double-wrapped), work wrapped stitch together with its wraps, w&t the following stitch.

Next row: Purl to first wrapped stitch (double-wrapped), work wrapped stitch together with its wraps, w&t the following stitch.

Repeat these last two rows until there is one double-wrapped stitch on either side of the heel. Knit to the first

double-wrapped stitch, pick up both wraps and knit them together with stitch, knit around the instep to the other double-wrapped stitch, working wraps together with the stitch. K16 (20) and place new beginning-of-round marker.

Leg
Knit 4 rounds. Change to Color B. Knit 1 round.
Note: You can carry the unused color up the back of the leg.
With Color A, knit 5 rounds.
With Color B, knit 1 round.
With Color A, knit 3 rounds.
With Color B, knit 2 rounds.
With Color A, knit 2 rounds.
With Color B, knit 3 rounds.
With Color A, knit 1 round.
With Color B, knit 3 rounds.
With Color A, knit 1 round. Break Color A.
With Color B, knit 8 rounds.
Work the *Shooting Stars Pattern* once. Knit 5 rounds. Work 1" (2.5cm) of k3, p1 ribbing. BO loosely.

Finishing
Weave in ends. Block if desired.

✦ *From the Designer* ✦

"*I've spent my whole life in Ohio until recently, when I relocated to the UK. Though I've left my home state, it is the place that has influenced me and left an indelible mark on me. No matter where I am in the world, Ohio's history is mine as well.*"

— *Joy Gerhardt*

Frank Lloyd Wright (1867 - 1959)

Widely revered as the greatest American architect of all time, Wisconsin-born Frank Lloyd Wright created "Prairie Style," an architectural style uniquely American. At a time when most buildings were designed with European influences, Wright, who was inspired by the "democratic spirit of America" designed buildings that honored the land and the people who lived on it.

Wright believed buildings should harmonize with their surroundings, and the interiors, landscapes and furnishings should be parts of the integrated whole. Wright masterfully incorporated 20th century advances in materials and technology while preserving the "soul" of architectural design. He changed the way we live.

> *What is architecture anyway? Is it the vast collection of the various buildings which have been built to please the varying tastes of the various lords of mankind? I think not. No, I know that architecture is life; or at least it is life itself taking form and therefore it is the truest record of life as it was lived in the world yesterday, as it is lived today or ever will be lived…So, architecture I know to be a Great Spirit. — Frank Lloyd Wright*

Throughout his career, Wright designed 532 buildings and interiors, more than 400 of which are still standing. Many of his masterpieces are in the Midwest. From 1889-1910, the first 20 years of his career, Wright lived in the village of Oak Park, Illinois, just outside Chicago. His home and studio are open to the public, restored to how they appeared in 1909, the last year he lived and worked there. The village also boasts more than 25 of his designs. Stop at the Frank Lloyd Wright Home & Studio to pick up a walking tour map and enjoy.

ᎠᏰᎧ Ohio River ᎠᏰᎧ

The Ohio River winds its way for almost a thousand miles through Pennsylvania, Ohio, West Virginia, Kentucky, Indiana, and Illinois. The river was the site of many Native American settlements, later became the boundary between European and Indian territories, and served as a major boundary between free and slave states.

Designer Rusty Theresa Morris was inspired by the sinuous path of the Ohio, represented here by the lovely twisting cables. Knit in a cozy worsted weight yarn, these socks knit up very quickly as well.

Sock Type: Cuff down

Finished Size: Adult Medium: Foot circumference 7½" (19cm); leg length to ankle 8" (20cm); foot length 8½" (21.5cm) or to fit (unstretched)

Project Gauge: 21 stitches and 28 rounds = 4" (10cm) in stockinette stitch, 36 stitches and 32 rounds = 4" (10cm) in *Sinuous River Cable Pattern*

Shopping List
Ella Rae *Classic Solids Superwash* (100% superwash wool, 219 yards/200m); 2 skeins Moody Blue #122
Size US 6 (4mm) double-pointed needles
Size US 7 (4.5mm) double-pointed needles
Stitch markers
Cable needle
Tapestry needle

Abbreviations
5 stitch crossover left (5CL)
Slip 3 stitches to a cable needle and hold in front, p2, then k3 from cable needle

5 stitch crossover right (5CR)
Slip 2 stitches to a cable needle and hold in back, k3, then p2 from cable needle

6 stitch crossover left (6CL)
Slip 3 stitches to a cable needle, and hold in front, k3, then k3 from cable needle

6 stitch crossover right (6CR)
Slip 3 stitches to a cable needle and hold in back, k3, then k3 from cable needle

Stitch Guide
Sinuous River Cable
Round 1: P2, k3, p4, k6, p5.
Round 2 and all even rounds: Knit the knits and purl the purls.
Round 3: P2, k3, p4, 6CL, p5.
Round 5: P2, 5CL, 5CR, 5CL, p3.
Round 7: P4, 6CR, p4, k3, p3.
Round 9: P2, 5CR, 5CL, 5CR, p3.
Round 10: Knit the knits and purl the purls.

Instructions
With smaller needles, CO 40 stitches. Join (being careful not to twist) and place marker for beginning of round. Work in 2x2 ribbing for 2" (5cm) or to desired length.
Next round: (K5, m1) around. 48 stitches.
Change to larger needles.
Leg round: (K2, work *Sinuous River Cable* across next 20 stitches, k2) twice.
Work rounds 1-10 of *Sinuous River Cable* pattern, then repeat rounds 3-10 twice more, and then work rounds 3-5 again.

Heel Flap
Setup for heel: (K2, work *Sinuous River Cable* round 2, k2), and stop here.
Row 1 (RS): K2, work in cable pattern as set across next 20 stitches, k2.
Row 2 (WS): P2, work in cable pattern as set across next 20 stitches, p2.
Continue until you have completed the current repeat of the *Sinuous River Cable Pattern*, and then work rows 3-10 once more, and then rows 3-5 again.

Heel Turn
Row 1 (RS): Sl1, k14, skp, K1, turn.
Row 2: Sl1, p7, p2tog, p1, turn.
Row 3: Sl1, knit to 1 stitch before gap, skp, k1, turn.
Row 4: Sl1, purl to one stitch before gap, p2tog, p1, turn.
Repeat rows 3- 4 until all stitches have been worked and 14 stitches remain.

Gusset
Needle 1: knit across heel stitches and pick up and knit 12 stitches on left side of sock; Needles 2 and 3: work pattern (starting *Sinuous River Cable* round 6) across instep stitches; Needle 4: pick up and knit 12 on right side and knit across 7 heel stitches. (19 stitches on Needles 1 and 4, 12 stitches on Needles 2 and 3).
Round 1: Needle 1: knit to last 3 stitches, k2tog,k1; Needles 2 and 3: continue in established pattern; Needle 4: k1, skp, knit to end of round.
Round 2: Needles 1 and 4: knit; Needles 2 and 3: continue in pattern.
Repeat these 2 rounds until 48 stitches remain.
Continue working in established pattern, knitting on sole stitches and pattern on instep, until 2" (5cm) shorter than desired length.

Toe
Round 1: Needle 1: knit to last 3 stitches, k2tog, k1; Needle 2: k1, skp, knit to end; Needle 3: knit to last 3 stitches, k2tog, k1; Needle 4: k1, skp, knit to end.
Round 2: Knit.
Repeat these 2 rounds until 16 stitches remain. Knit stitches from Needle 1 onto Needle 4. Cut yarn.

Finishing
Graft toe closed using Kitchener Stitch. (See page 91). Weave in ends. Block if desired.

Sinuous River Cable Pattern

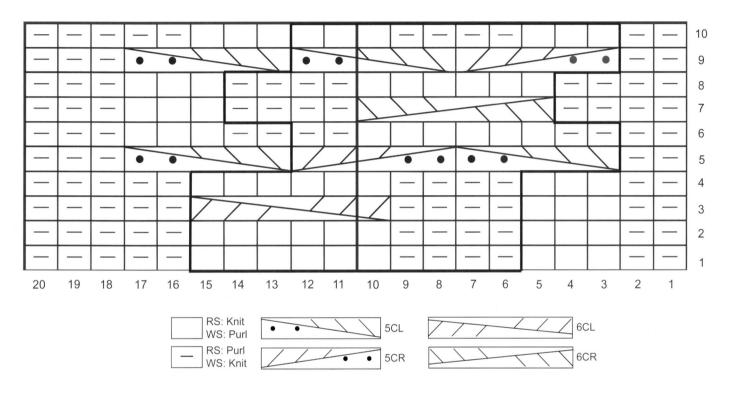

							5CL					6CL
RS: Knit / WS: Purl			• •									
RS: Purl / WS: Knit				• •		5CR						6CR

✦ From the Designer ✦

"I live in Cincinnati, where the Ohio River separates Ohio from Kentucky by a narrow swath of water. I love how the river bends, twists and turns throughout its journey, so narrow in some places that you can easily swim across from one state to another."

— Rusty Theresa Morris

Chicago-Style Hot Dogs

There are only two places in the world where I order hot dogs — New York City from street vendors and Chicago from anywhere I can get them! Though I was born in Chicago, we moved when I was six. My son went to college in Chi-Town and reintroduced me to the city, including Chicago dogs. I order mine without the hot peppers as I'm kind of a weenie (pun intended), but my son assures me that the they add just the right amount of heat. I'll take his word for it.

Directions

Steam, boil or grill hot dogs. For safety, they should reach an internal temperature of 170°. Steam the buns.

To assemble, place dog in the bun. Tuck tomato slices inside the bun on one side of the dog, cucumber slices on the other. Add toppings in this order: mustard, sweet green relish, onion, pickle, sport peppers, and celery salt.

Shopping List

8 Vienna or Hebrew National all-beef franks

8 poppy seed buns

Yellow mustard (with or without horseradish)

Sweet green pickle relish (bright green if you can find it)

Chopped onion

Sliced tomato

Sliced cucumber

8 kosher pickle spears

16 sport peppers (pickled Serrano peppers)

Celery salt

Sedona, Arizona

Southwest

Some of the world's most dramatic scenery is found across the deserts and canyons of the American Southwest. It's impossible to avoid being awed and inspired by the striations of color that build along the plateaus and rock formations, giving them their distinctive painted look. It's no wonder the area attracts so many artists and writers.

No trip to the Southwest is complete without a visit to the Georgia O'Keeffe Museum in Santa Fe. The museum attracts over 2 million visitors a year and is the only museum in the world dedicated to an internationally known female American artist. The museum owns over 1,000 of her works, the largest collection in the world. It also exhibits many photos and writings by O'Keeffe and her friends, documenting her journey from New York City artist, to her budding love affair with the Southwest, and finally her life in New Mexico, where she uniquely captured the stark beauty of the landscape, architecture and plants.

The Southwestern states may be newcomers to the Union, but it is an ancient land, inhabited by humans for over 1,200 years. Ancient Pueblo peoples ruled the land, creating irrigation canals and building cliff dwellings that survive today. The best place to explore this history is Chaco Canyon, New Mexico, a UNESCO World Heritage Site dedicated to the preservation of this once major cultural center of the Ancient Pueblo peoples. Until the 19th century, these buildings were the largest structures in North America.

A sense of untamed wilderness lives on in much of the landscape. Many areas are largely uninhabited, other than by the bighorn sheep, bobcats, coyote, bear, deer, foxes, bison and mountain lions that make the Southwest their homes.

This is the land of larger-than-life figures like Jesse James, Wyatt Earp, Annie Oakley and Buffalo Bill. The romance of the "Wild West" still fascinates us, even if it is largely fictional. The image of the ruggedly handsome cowboy, hat dipped low, heading off into the sunset on his trusty horse, is maybe *the* iconic all-American image. And it figures in a lot of dreams and fantasies. Or so I've heard....

Grand Canyon

The Grand Canyon is one of the seven natural wonders of the world, and the only one in the United States. Carved by the Colorado River over the course of at least 17 million years, it measures 18 miles at its widest, and its deepest point is over a mile below the surface. For 277 miles, its buttes and crags provide an awe-inspiring natural color show.

Designer Sara Elizabeth Schmidt took inspiration from the canyon to create these beautiful socks. With their warm colorway and a design that flows together and apart, the socks pay tribute to the changing textures of the canyon surfaces. ¡Qué hermosos!

Sock Type: Cuff down on double-pointed needles

Finished Size: Adult Medium: Foot circumference 7½" (19cm); leg length to ankle 8" (20cm); foot length 8¾" (22cm) (unstretched)

Project Gauge: 32 stitches and 42 rounds = 4" (10cm) in stockinette stitch; 34 stitches and 42 rounds = 4" in *Canyon Lace Pattern*

Shopping List
Lorna's Laces *Shepherd Sock* (80% superwash merino wool, 20% nylon, 430 yards/393m); 1 skein Brick
Size US 0 (2mm) double-pointed needles (set of 4)
Stitch marker
Tapestry needle

Stitch Guide
Twisted Rib
Every round: *K1 tbl, p1; repeat from * to end.

Canyon Lace Pattern
Round 1: *P4, k2tog, yo, k2, k2tog, yo, k1, p4; repeat from * to end.
Round 2 and all even rounds: Knit.
Round 3: *P3, k2tog, yo, k2, k2tog, yo, k1, yo, ssk, p3; repeat from * to end.
Round 5: *P2, k2tog, yo, k2, k2tog, yo, k3, yo, ssk, p2; repeat from * to end.
Round 7: *P1, k2tog, yo, k2, k2tog, yo, k1, yo, ssk, k2, yo, ssk, p1; repeat from * to end.

Round 9: *K2tog, yo, k2, k2tog, yo, k3, yo, ssk, k2, yo, ssk; repeat from * to end.
Round 11: *K2, yo, ssk, k3, k2tog, yo, k2, k2tog, yo, k2; repeat from * to end.
Round 13: *K3, yo, ssk, k1, k2tog, yo, k2, k2tog, yo, k3; repeat from * to end.
Round 15: *K4, yo, sk2p, yo, k2, k2tog, yo, k4; repeat from * to end.
Round 16: Knit.
Repeat rounds 1-16 for pattern.

Instructions
CO 60 stitches. Divide stitches evenly between 3 needles. Join for knitting in the round. Work 2" (5cm) in *Twisted Rib.* Work 5 repeats of *Canyon Lace Pattern* or until desired length to ankle.

Heel Flap
Note: Heel flap is worked back and forth over 30 stitches, beginning with a WS row.
Row 1 (WS): (Sl1, p1) across all 30 stitches, turn.
Row 2 (RS): Sl1, k29, turn.
Repeat rows 1-2 fourteen times more.

Heel Turn
Row 1 (WS): P20, p2tog, turn.
Row 2 (RS): Sl1, k10, ssk, turn.
Row 3: Sl1, p10, p2tog, turn.
Repeat rows 2-3 seven times more, then work row 2 once more. 12 stitches remain.

Gusset
Knit across remaining heel stitches. Pick up and knit 16 stitches along first side of heel flap (Needle 1); work in pattern across instep stitches (Needle 2); pick up and knit 16 stitches along next side of heel flap, k6 from heel (Needle 3); slip last 6 stitches to Needle 1. Needle 1 now marks the beginning of the round.
Round 1 (decrease round): Needle 1: knit to last 3 stitches, k2tog, k1; Needle 2: keep in pattern; Needle 3: k1, ssk, knit to end.
Round 2: Needle 1: knit; Needle 2: keep in pattern; Needle 3: knit.

Repeat these 2 rounds six times more. (60 stitches). Work even in pattern until foot measures 1½" (4cm) shorter than desired length.

Toe
Round 1 (decrease round): Needle 1: knit to last 3 stitches, k2tog, k1; Needle 2: k1, ssk, knit to last 3 stitches, k2tog, k1; Needle 3: k1, ssk, knit to end.
Round 2: Knit.
Repeat these 2 rounds four times more, then work decrease round five times. (20 stitches remain). Knit stitches from Needle 1 onto Needle 3.

Finishing
Graft toe closed using Kitchener Stitch. (See page 91). Weave in ends. Block if desired.

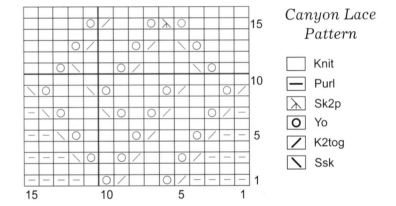

Canyon Lace Pattern

☐	Knit
—	Purl
⋋	Sk2p
O	Yo
╱	K2tog
╲	Ssk

The Ancient Pueblo Peoples

In 1888, European explorers stumbled upon an amazing discovery — an abandoned city carved into the cliffs of what is now Mesa Verde, Colorado. The city included thousands of intact ancient structures. So far, more than 600 dwellings have been mapped and an additional 4,100 archaeological sites have been discovered.

Scientists believe the structures were built around 1190 A.D., while cultivation of the land atop the mesas predates the cliff dwellings by 600 years. The settlement at Mesa Verde includes everything from a one-room storage shed to the 150-room "Cliff Palace" built into the rock. The mesa was abandoned less than 100 years later, leaving archaeologists to ponder the mystery surrounding the abandonment of the settlement.

The Ancient Pueblo peoples left behind a plethora of artifacts that remained preserved by the dry desert heat. Discarded tools, baskets and pottery sat undisturbed; petroglyphs still decorated the walls. Scholars and scientists began piecing together theories of what had happened to cause the Ancient Pueblo peoples to abandon their homes. For many years, they believed a major drought was the cause of the migration south to less arid regions in Arizona and New Mexico. Evidence discovered through new climatological studies seems to indicate that the Great Drought was less severe than previously thought and may have only been one factor in the migration. Anthropologists now believe that religious schism or war may have been the main motivation.

Scientists will continue to argue how this once great society crumbled. There's no debate, however, that the magic of Mesa Verde National Park will stay with you forever.

Fresh Salsa & Guacamole

Southwestern cuisine has been heavily influenced by both Mexican and Spanish cooking. The Americanized fusion, called Tex-Mex, is one of the most popular and flavorful cuisines in the United States. Fast food chain versions are nothing like fresh Tex-Mex, which celebrates vibrant veggies and spices. This fresh salsa and guacamole are frequent requests from my Tex-Mex-loving family, especially on game days. Use only fresh ingredients for this and you'll never buy bottled salsa or prepared guacamole again.

Directions

Salsa: Chop tomatoes coarsely. Add the chopped red onions, spring onions, garlic, cilantro, vinegar, salt and jalapenos (optional). Cover and refrigerate. Serve chilled.

Makes about 1 quart.

Guacamole: Coarsely chop one avocado and set aside. In a medium bowl, mash the remaining two avocados with a fork. Add the fresh salsa one tablespoon at a time, to taste. Fold in the chopped avocado. Squeeze the lime half over the top and sprinkle with two pinches of coarsely ground salt. Serve immediately with tortilla chips or toasted slices of baguette.

Shopping List

Salsa

4 large tomatoes

1 medium red onion, chopped

1 large spring onion, chopped

2 Tbl fresh cilantro, chopped

2 garlic cloves, minced

2 jalapeno peppers, seeded and finely chopped (optional)

2 Tbl red wine vinegar

1 tsp salt

Guacamole

3 avocados

Salsa (above), to taste

½ fresh lime

2 pinches coarsely ground salt

Oregon Orchard

Northwest

The American Northwest is the lushest area of the country. The frequent rain in Seattle and Portland may be the subject of many jokes, but the resultant deep green vegetation is truly breathtaking. And that kind of weather is perfect for knitting.

The cool climate is also great for growing pears, apples and the best berries in the country. My favorite way to spend a summer day in Oregon is to load up with fresh berries from a roadside stand — blackberries, marionberries, strawberries, blueberries and raspberries — and then picnic until I can't fit another berry in my belly. These fresh-from-the-farm fruits have little resemblance, taste-wise, to what we get in the grocery store. It's "berry magic."

I was enchanted when I visited Portland one winter and it was snowing on the beach. Snowing. On the beach. If the only beaches you've seen are the wide, sandy, sunny, warm-water kind on the East Coast, you owe it to yourself to visit the wild, rocky shores of Oregon and Washington. But if you plan to go into the water, bring a wetsuit in summer and drysuit the rest of the year because, baby, the water's cold. Brrrrrrrrr.

The beautiful San Juan Islands, off the coast of Washington, are the warmest winter spot in the Pacific Northwest. The northernmost point in the lower 48 states, these islands are famous for whale watching. Between March and November, you can take a boat tour and see orcas up close and personal.

Further inland, both Washington and Oregon have world-class wine-growing regions. Southeastern Oregon, particularly the area around Medford, is a foodie's paradise, with wineries, artisan cheese makers and chocolatiers. Washington state has almost 700 wineries, many clustered in the Yakima Valley and the areas around Puget Sound and Walla Walla.

After all that food and wine, work it off with a hike along the Columbia River Gorge, or skiing Mt. Hood or Mt. Bachelor. Or say "the heck with it" and spend the rest of your trip visiting the fabulous yarn stores.

✤ Willamette River ✤

Eighty percent of Oregonians live within twenty miles of the Willamette River, which runs through both Portland and Salem. Archaeological finds show that the river valley has been populated for at least 10,000 years. It wasn't until the 19th century that Europeans settled the valley, with the Oregon Trail ending at the mouth of the river.

Designer Allison Isaac lives near the Willamette River in Newburg and designed these socks to honor both it and the majestic Cascade Mountains that stand watch over the area and whose peaks inspired the design of the beaded cuff.

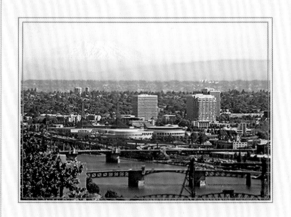

Sock Type: Cuff down with magic loop

Finished Size: Adult Medium: Foot circumference 7¾" (19.5cm); leg length to ankle 6" (15cm); foot length 8" (10cm) (unstretched)

Project Gauge: 32 stitches and 44 rounds = 4" (10 cm) in stockinette stitch; 32 stitches and 44 rounds = 4" (10cm) in *Winding River Lace Pattern*

Shopping List
Cascade Yarns *Heritage Solids* (75% Merino Superwash, 25% Nylon, 437 yards/400m); 1 skein Turquoise #5626
Size US 1.5 (2.5mm) 40" (100cm) circular needle for magic loop
176 8/0 seed beads (sample uses Czech seed beads, Caribbean Blue mix)
Tool of choice for stringing beads onto yarn (crochet hook or beading needle)
Tapestry needle

Stitch Guide
Bead: Slide bead close to stitch, knit stitch pushing bead to front leg of stitch on RS of work. On next round, knit beaded stitch through the back loop.

Winding River Lace Pattern (Chart C)
Round 1: *Yo, k2, ssk, k4; repeat from * to end.
Round 2-3: Knit.
Round 4: *K1, yo, k2, ssk, k3; repeat from * to end.
Rounds 5-6: Knit.

Round 7: *K2, yo, k2, ssk, k2; repeat from * to end.
Rounds 8-9: Knit.
Round 10: *K3, yo, k2, ssk, k1; repeat from * to end.
Rounds 11-12: Knit.
Round 13: *K4, yo, k2, ssk; repeat from * to end.
Rounds 14-15: Knit.
Round 16: *K4, k2tog, k2, yo; repeat from * to end.

Rounds 17-18: Knit.
Round 19: *K3, k2tog, k2, yo, k1; repeat from * to end.
Rounds 20-21: Knit.
Round 22: *K2, k2tog, k2, yo, k2; repeat from * to end.
Rounds 23-24: Knit.
Round 25: *K1, k2tog, k2, yo, k3; repeat from * to end.
Rounds 26-27: Knit.
Round 28: *K2tog, k2, yo, k4; repeat from * to end.
Rounds 29-30: Knit.
Repeat rounds 1-30 for pattern.

Instructions

For each sock, pre-string 88 beads onto yarn.
CO 64 stitches, 32 on each side of magic loop needle. Pm to mark beginning of round. Knit 7 rounds, allowing the work to curl. Work 7 rounds of 1x1 rib.
Starting with a knit round, work 4 rounds garter stitch (knit one round, purl one round).

Left sock only: Work Chart A across first side of needle, then Chart B across second side of needle.

Right sock only: Work Chart B across first side of needle, then Chart A across second side of needle.

Both socks: Work all 27 rounds of Charts A & B. Knit one more round after chart is completed. Starting with a knit round, work 5 rounds of garter stitch. Work Chart C eight times around sock. Work chart once through, or until desired length.

Heel set up
Note: This stitch rearranging is necessary to put Mt. Hood (Chart A) on the side of the sock instead of the front/back.
K16, turn, sl1 pwise wyif, p31. Rearrange stitches now to put 32 stitches just worked (including the slipped stitch) onto first side of needle and the stitches left unworked, which will become the instep stitches, onto the second side of needle.

Heel flap
Turn so that RS is facing.
Row 1: Sl1 kwise wyib, k1, *sl1 pwise wyib, k1; repeat from * to end.

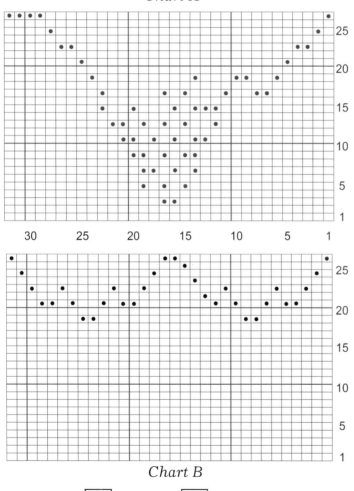

Chart A

Chart B

Knit   ● Place bead

Row 2: Sl1 pwise wyif, purl to end.
Repeat rows 1-2 until you have 32 rows total.

Turn heel
Row 1: Sl1 kwise wyib, k17, ssk, k1, turn.
Row 2: Sl1 pwise wyif, p5, p2tog, p1, turn.
Row 3: Sl1 kwise wyib, knit to 1 stitch before gap from turn, ssk, k1 turn.
Row 4: Sl1 pwise wyif, purl to 1 stitch before gap from turn, p2tog, p1 turn.
Repeat rows 3-4 until all stitches are worked, ending with a row 4. (18 stitches remain).

Gusset
Sl1 kwise wyib, knit across heel stitches, pick up 16 stitches along side of heel flap, then 2 stitches in gap between flap and instep to prevent holes, work next round of Chart C across instep stitches, pick up 2 stitches in gap between heel flap and instep, pick up 16 stitches in other side of heel flap, k9, pm to mark new beginning of round.
Round 1: Knit to instep, work next round of Chart C across instep, knit to end of round.
Round 2: Knit to 3 stitches before end of needle, k2tog, k1, work next round of Chart C across instep, k1, ssk, knit to end of round.
Repeat rounds 1-2 until 32 sole stitches remain.
Continue working Chart C on instep and plain stockinette stitch on sole until 2" (5cm) shorter than desired length. Knit to end of sole; this is the new beginning of round.

Toe (discontinue Chart C)
Round 1: *K1, ssk, knit to 3 stitches before end of needle, k2tog, k1; repeat from * to end.
Round 2: Knit.
Repeat these 2 rounds until 20 stitches remain on each side.
Repeat round 1 only until 8 stitches remain on each side.

Finishing
Graft toe closed using Kitchener Stitch. (See page 91).
Weave in ends.

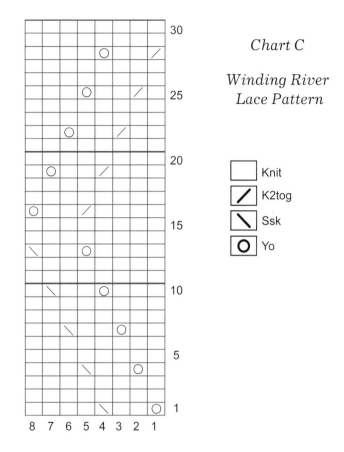

Chart C

Winding River
Lace Pattern

	Knit
/	K2tog
\	Ssk
O	Yo

✳ *From the Designer* ✳

"The beaded cuff is inspired by beautiful Mt. Hood, visible from most areas of the Willamette Valley. The color of the yarn and the beads I chose remind me of the Pacific Ocean, and the stitch pattern is representative of the ripples of the Willamette River, which runs along the edge of my town."

— *Allison Isaac*

❧ Sweet Onion ❧

*W*alla Walla and the surrounding area
is heaven for food and wine aficionados.
Vineyards, fertile soil and gorgeous produce
have given rise to extraordinary restaurants
and wineries. "Farm-to-table" isn't a fad
here — it's a way of life.

Sweet onions grow in abundance in
the area and this sock by designer Susan
Moskwa is proof that design inspiration can
come from anywhere, including your own
refrigerator. The cable design evokes the
distinctive shape of sweet onion bulbs. This
is one way you can enjoy onions without
worrying about your breath.

Sock Type: Cuff down

Finished Sizes: Adult S (M, L): Foot circumference:
8 (9, 10½)" (20 [22.5, 26]cm); leg length: 7" (18cm);
foot length: 9 (9½, 10)" (23 [24, 25.5]cm) or to fit
(unstretched)

Project Gauge: 42 stitches and 51 rounds = 4" (10cm)
in stockinette stitch; 41 stitches and 50 rounds = 4"
(10cm) in *Onion Cable Pattern*

Shopping List
Lorna's Laces *Shepherd Sock* (80% superwash wool,
20% nylon, 215 yards/197m); 1 skein Silence
Size US 1 (2.25mm) needles (double-pointed needles
or 2 circular needles)
Stitch markers
Cable needle
Tapestry needle

Abbreviations
C2B - Slip one stitch to cable needle and hold in back;
knit one, then knit stitch from cable needle
C2F- Slip one stitch to cable needle and hold in front;
knit one, then knit stitch from cable needle
C2BKP - Slip one stitch to cable needle and hold in
back; knit one, then purl stitch from cable needle
C2FPK - Slip one stitch to cable needle and hold in
front; purl one, then knit stitch from cable needle

Instructions

Loosely CO 64 (72, 84) stitches. Join for knitting in the round, making sure not to twist. Place marker.

Cuff

Work round 1 of *Onion Cable Pattern* chart around. Repeat round 1 around until cuff is 1" (2.5cm) long.

Leg

Work rows 2-25 (29, 33) of *Onion Cable Pattern* twice, ending after row 25 (29, 33). Don't forget to omit round 1 the second time through.

Heel flap

The heel flap is worked back and forth over the last 32 (36, 42) stitches; hold instep stitches aside (on cable or waste yarn) while working heel flap. If you're comfortable cabling on both the RS and the WS of your work, choose the decorative heel instructions below; if not, work the simple heel.

Decorative heel (shown)

Starting on the WS, *Sl1, continue *Onion Cable Pattern* as established across heel stitches. Repeat from * through row 14 (14, 16) of the *Onion Cable Pattern*. On the next row: *Sl1, work stitches as they appear; repeat from * until heel flap is 28 (28, 30) rows long, ending with a RS row.

Simple heel

Row 1 (WS): Sl1, p1; work stitches as they appear (k the knit, p the purl) until last 2 heel stitches, p2.

Row 2 (RS): Sl1, k1; slip all knit stitches and purl all purl stitches until last 2 heel stitches, k2.

Repeat these 2 rows thirteen (thirteen, fourteen) times.

Heel turn

Row 1 (WS): Sl1, k21 (23, 27), turn work.

Row 2 (RS): Sl1, p11 (11, 13), turn.

Row 3: Sl1, knit to 1 stitch before the gap created by turning on the previous row, k2tog the stitches on either side of the gap, k1, turn.

Row 4: Sl1, purl to 1 stitch before the gap created by turning on the previous row, p2tog the stitches on either side of the gap, p1, turn.

Repeat rows 3-4 until all heel stitches have been worked.

Gusset

Knit across heel stitches. Pick up and knit 15 (15, 16) stitches along the edge of the heel flap. This location (immediately before the first instep stitch) is now the beginning of the round.

Round 1: Continue *Onion Cable Pattern* as established across instep (you should be on round 2 of the *Onion Cable Pattern*. Pick up and knit 15 (15, 16) stitches along the other edge of the heel flap. Purl to end of round.

Round 2: Work *Onion Cable Pattern* across instep, purl to end of round.

Round 3: Work *Onion Cable Pattern* to end of instep stitches, ssp, purl to last 2 stitches, p2tog.

Repeat rounds 2-3 until 64 (72, 84) stitches remain.

Next round: Work *Onion Cable Pattern* across instep, purl across sole. Repeat this round until sock measures 7½ (8, 8½)" from back of heel, or 1½" less than desired length.

Toe

Round 1: K1, ssk, knit until last 3 instep stitches, k2tog, k1; p1, p2tog, purl until last 3 sole stitches, p2tog, p1.

Round 2: Work all stitches as they appear.

Repeat these 2 rounds until 28 (36, 48) stitches remain, then repeat round 1 once more.

Finishing

Graft toe closed using Kitchener Stitch. (See page 91). Weave in ends. Block if desired.

✶ *From the Designer* ✶

"*The Walla Walla sweet onion is Washington's state vegetable, named after the city of Walla Walla in the southeastern part of the state. The round shapes and the color of this design were inspired by my hometown's famous onions.*"

— *Susan Moskwa*

Size
Small

**Instep/Front of
Leg Stitches**

**Sole/Back of
Leg Stitches**

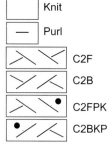

	Knit
—	Purl
	C2F
	C2B
	C2FPK
	C2BKP

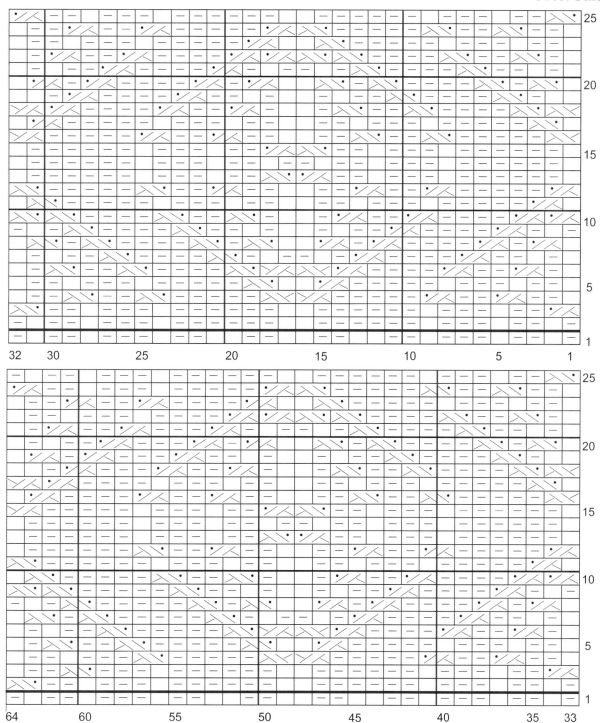

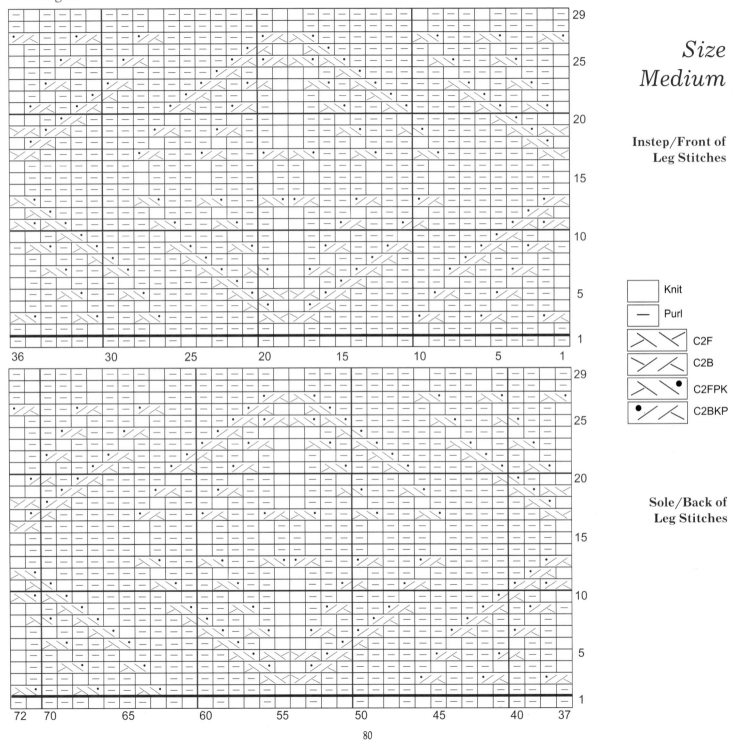

Size
Medium

**Instep/Front of
Leg Stitches**

		Knit
—		Purl
		C2F
		C2B
		C2FPK
		C2BKP

**Sole/Back of
Leg Stitches**

Size Large

Instep/Front of Leg Stitches

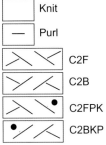

Knit

— Purl

C2F

C2B

• C2FPK

• C2BKP

Sole/Back of Leg Stitches

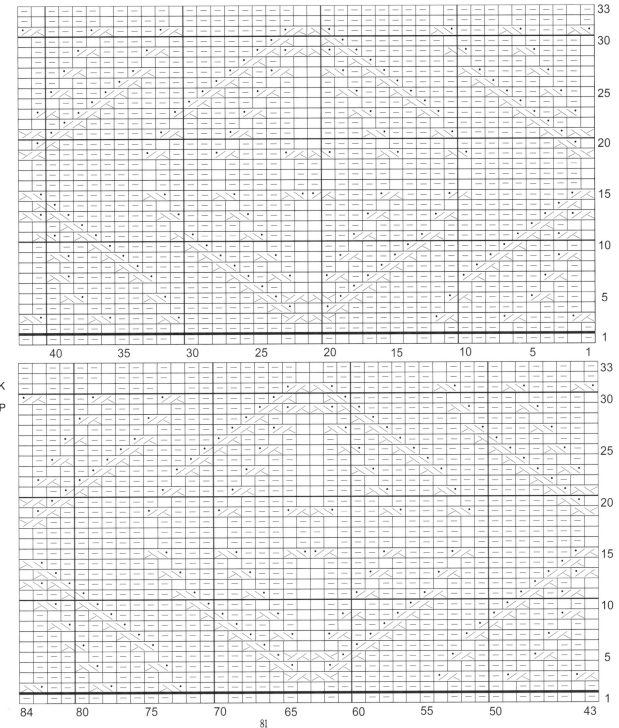

⚜ Big Sky ⚜

One of my favorite vacations was a two-week road trip with my son through Glacier National Park in Montana and Grand Teton National Park in Wyoming. I was awestruck by the mountain scenery and wide open skies.

Designer Kim Haesemeyer has lived in Montana for 15 years, and pays tribute to her adopted home with these socks that celebrate the "Big Sky" state. The leg is worked back and forth in a simple intarsia pattern, then seamed up and knit in the round for the rest of the sock.

Sock Type: Cuff down

Finished Sizes: Women's Small (women's shoe size 6-7); Women's Medium/Men's Small (women's shoe size 8-9; men's shoe size 6-7); Women's Large/Men's Medium (women's shoe size 10-11; men's shoe size 8-9); Men's Large (men's shoe size 10-11); foot circumference: 8 (8, 8½, 9)" (20.5 [20.5, 21.5, 23]cm); leg length: 8½" (21.5cm); foot length: 9 (9½, 10½, 11½)" (23 [24, 26.5, 29]cm) or to fit (unstretched)

Project Gauge: 32 stitches and 44 rounds = 4" (10cm) in stockinette stitch with smaller needles

Shopping List
Berroco *Comfort Sock* (50% Super Fine Nylon, 50% Super Fine Acrylic, 447 yards/412m); 1 skein each Hari Hari #1811 (MC) and Pearl #1702 (CC)
Size US 2 (2.75mm) needles, 2 straight and 4 double-pointed
Size US 4 (3.5mm) double-pointed needles
Stitch marker
Tapestry needle
Waste yarn of similar weight

Instructions
Leg
With MC and smaller straight needles, provisionally CO 66 (66, 70, 74) stitches. Work in stockinette stitch for 3 rows, beginning with a

purl row. Continuing with MC, k7 (7, 8, 9) stitches, work 20 stitches of *Cloud Chart* beginning with row 1, k12 (12, 14, 16) with MC, work 20 stitches of *Cloud Chart* (row 1 again), k7 (7, 8, 9) with MC to end of row. Continue working as established until all 24 rows of chart have been worked. Place stitches on waste yarn. Break yarns, leaving a long length of MC to seam. Seam the side edges with mattress stitch, one stitch from each edge in the seam and keeping all stitches on waste yarn (including the seam stitches). Evenly distribute the stitches on 3 smaller double-pointed needles with the 4th needle as the working needle. Place marker at the seam to indicate the beginning of the round.

Round 1 (MC): K2tog, knit to last 2 stitches of round, k2tog. 64 (64, 68, 72) stitches remain.

Rounds 2-4 (MC): Knit.

Rounds 5-6 (CC): Knit.

Rounds 7-10 (MC): Knit.

Repeat rounds 5-10 twice more. Repeat rounds 5-6 once. Break CC.

Cloud Chart

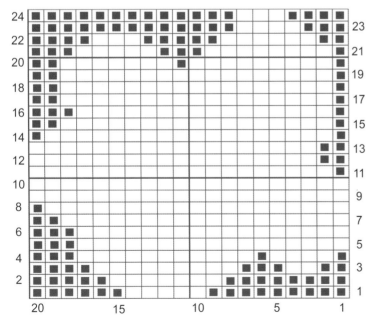

Heel Flap

Work entire heel in MC.

Row 1: K16 (16, 17, 18).

Turn work. P32 (32, 34, 36) stitches, removing marker. Total heel stitches: 32 (32, 34, 36)

Divide the remaining 32 (32, 34, 36) stitches evenly on two needles and hold for later.

With the 32 (32, 34, 36) stitches, proceed to work the heel flap as follows:

Row 1 (RS): *Sl1 pwise wyib, k1; repeat from * to end of row.

Row 2 (WS): Sl1 pwise, purl to end of row.

Work these 2 rows fifteen (fifteen, sixteen, seventeen) more times for 32 (32, 34, 36) rows total, ending with a WS row.

Heel

Row 1: Sl1 pwise, k18 (18, 19, 21), ssk, k1, turn.

Row 2: Sl1 pwise, p7 (7, 7, 9), p2tog, p1, turn.

Row 3: Sl1 pwise, knit to 1 stitch before gap, ssk, k1, turn.

Row 4: Sl1 pwise, purl to 1 stitch before gap, p2tog, p1, turn.

Repeat rows 3-4 until 20 (20, 22, 24) stitches remain, ending with a WS row. Proceed with last two rows of heel flap as follows:

Row 1 (RS): Sl1 pwise, knit to last two stitches, ssk.
Row 2 (WS): Sl1 pwise, purl to last two stitches, p2tog. 18 (18, 20, 22) stitches remain.

Gusset

Next round (RS): With MC, k18 (18, 20, 22) heel stitches. Continue with Needle 1 and MC, to the left of the working yarn along the left side of the sock flap, pick up and knit 16 (16, 17, 18) stitches in the loops created by the slipped stitches along the heel flap. Continue to pick up and knit one more gutter stitch for 17 (17, 18, 19) stitches total. With Needle 2, knit across the 32 (32, 34, 36) stitches on the other two needles, working them onto one needle. With Needle 3, pick up and knit the gutter stitch and an additional 16 (16, 17, 18) stitches in the loops created by the slipped stitches along the heel flap for 17 (17, 18, 19) stitches total. Knit 9 (9, 10, 11) of the heel stitches from Needle 1. This is the new beginning of round. Needle 1 has half of the heel stitches and first set of new stitches, Needle 2 is the instep, and Needle 3 has the second set of new stitches and the other half of the heel stitches. Needle 1: 26 (26, 28, 30); Needle 2 (instep): 32 (32, 34, 36); Needle 3: 26 (26, 28, 30).

Gusset Decreases

Resume working 4 rounds MC and 2 rounds CC, keeping in mind one round of MC was worked when picking up stitches for the gusset, while at the same time working the gusset decrease as follows:

Round 1: Needle 1: knit to last 3 stitches of needle, k2tog, k1; Needle 2 [instep]: knit; Needle 3: k1, ssk, knit to end.
Round 2: Knit all three needles.

Repeat rounds 1-2 nine (nine, ten, eleven) more times. 64 (64, 68, 72) stitches with 16 (16, 17, 18) stitches on both Needle 1 and Needle 3 and 32 (32, 34, 36) on Needle 2.

Foot

Work in stockinette stitch and established stripe pattern until sock measures 7¼ (7¾, 8¾, 9¾)" [18.5 (19.5, 22, 25) cm] from back of heel or 1¾" (4.5cm) from desired length, ending with round worked in MC. Break CC. Work with MC for the remainder of the sock.

Toe

Round 1: Needle 1: knit to last 3 stitches, k2tog; k1; Needle 2: k1, ssk, knit to last 3 stitches, k2tog, k1; Needle 3: k1, ssk, knit to end.
Round 2: Knit all 3 needles.

Repeat rounds 1-2 six more times. Work round 1 only five times. 4 (4, 5, 6) stitches on Needle 1 and Needle 3 and 8 (8, 10, 12) stitches on Needle 2. 16 (16, 20, 24) stitches total. Using Needle 3, knit the 4 (4, 5, 6) stitches on Needle 1. Needle 2 has 8 (8, 10, 12) stitches and Needle 3 has 8 (8, 10, 12) stitches with the working yarn at the end of Needle 3. Break yarn, leaving long tail.

Finishing

Graft toe closed using Kitchener Stitch. (See page 91).

Cuff

Unzip the provisional cast on and divide stitches evenly on 3 smaller double-pointed needles with the 4th needle as the working needle. Place marker at seam to indicate the beginning of the round.

With MC, work decrease round as follows:

Decrease round: K2tog, knit to last 2 stitches of round, k2tog. 64 (64, 68, 72) stitches remain.

Slip Stitch Corrugated Ribbing

Note: Two rounds are required for one complete round of corrugated ribbing. very other stitch is worked on each round, alternating one round MC and one round CC. When changing colors at the beginning/end of a round make sure to twist the old and new yarns to prevent a hole in the fabric. Change to larger needles.

Round 1 (MC): *K2, sl2 wyib; repeat from * to end of round.
Round 2 (CC): *Sl2 wyib, k2; repeat from * to end of round.
Round 3 (MC): *K2, sl2 wyib; repeat from * to end of round.
Round 4 (CC): *(Wyib sl2, p2] ; rep from * to end of round.
Repeat rounds 3-4 for 1" (2.5cm). Break CC.

Rolled Cuff Edge

Switch to smaller needles. With MC, work in stockinette stitch for 1" (2.5cm). BO with larger needles.
Weave in ends. Block if desired.

Tips

- Begin toe decreases when sock is approximately 1¾" (4.5cm) from desired finished length.

- The leg of the sock with the cloud chart is worked flat on the straight needles, beginning with a provisional cast on. After the chart has been worked, the fabric is seamed and worked in the round from that point.

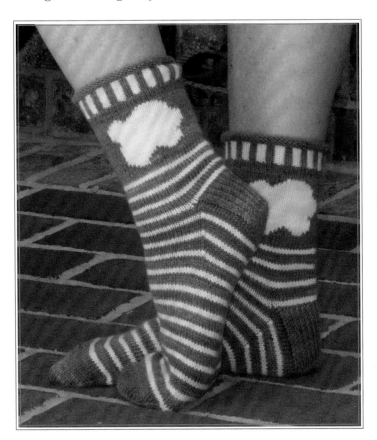

✳ From the Designer ✳

"After my third child was born, I taught myself to knit from a kit I purchased on clearance. Soon after that, I started designing. Absolutely anything can inspire me. I love to look at the color combinations and designs in nature. You can follow my knitting journey on my blog at bigskyyarnsandcrafts.com."

— Kim Haesemeyer

Glacier National Park

My favorite U.S. national park is Glacier National Park in Montana. With 740 miles of trails, glaciers, lakes, historic lodges, and summer huckleberries, what's not to love?

The highlight of the park is the "Going to the Sun Road," fifty miles of indescribable scenery. Bighorn sheep, waterfalls and Jackson Glacier are all visible from the road. The drive is not for the faint of heart, so if you want to just relax and enjoy the view, take a tour in a classic open-top red bus.

The summer months in Glacier mean huckleberries. Huckleberry-stuffed french toast is reason enough to make the trek. You'll see huckleberry ice cream, syrup, preserves, pie, shortcake and chocolates. Take my advice and try them all.

For a special trip, stay at one of the park's six historic lodges. Most of the inns were constructed by the Great Northern Railroad, which laid tracks into Northwest Montana in the 1890s. The lodges were built in the early 1900s to house tourists arriving by rail. My favorite is the Glacier Park Lodge, called "Big Tree Lodge" by the Indians, as the reception area features 60 exposed ancient tree trunks, 36 - 42" in diameter, 40 feet long and most still retaining their bark.

Glacier National Park backs right up to the Canadian border and continues across to Waterton Peace Park on the other side. The historic Prince of Wales Lodge at Waterton features a wall of glass and a jaw-dropping view when you enter. Go for lunch or afternoon tea and save some time to walk around the charming town. If you see bumbleberry pie — a yummy mix of huckleberries, raspberries, blackberries and blueberries — on any chalkboard menus, please pick me up a slice? Thanks!

Berry-Stuffed French Toast

My favorite time to visit my in-laws in Oregon is summer, when there's a veritable berry boom. My husband and I stop at farmer's markets and roadside stands where we stuff ourselves to bursting with berries every day. I always pick up some homemade preserves to take home and get a taste of that summer flavor year-round. I like to use marionberry or blackberry, but you can make this french toast with any preserve you like.

Directions

If using an unsliced loaf of bread, using a bread knife, cut sixteen 1/2" slices from the loaf. Preheat oven to 300°. Place bread on wire racks set on baking sheets. Bake bread until slightly dried on the outside, but still moist on the inside, turning over after five minutes. Remove bread from oven and let cool on racks until cool enough to touch. Reduce oven heat to warm.

Match bread slices up as if for sandwiches. Spread the insides of both pieces of each sandwich with softened cream cheese. Spread one side with preserves and re-assemble the sandwich.

Whisk all wet ingredients together in a large bowl until very well blended. Heat 2 Tbl of butter with 1 tsp of cooking oil in a large fry pan over medium-low heat. Place one sandwich in the bowl for about ten seconds, turn it over, and soak second side for ten seconds. Lift from the bowl and transfer to the heated pan. Repeat for as many that will fit without crowding. Cook until golden brown, flip and cook second side. Transfer to a baking sheet and keep warm in the oven. Wipe out pan and add more butter and oil between batches.

Serve warm, dusted with confectioners sugar and serving warm maple syrup separately, if desired.

Shopping List

16 slices hearty white sandwich bread or 1 loaf of unsliced country-style white bread

2 c. whole milk, warmed

3 large egg yolks

4 Tbl light brown sugar

1 tsp ground cinnamon

3 Tbl melted unsalted butter

¼ tsp salt

1 Tbl pure vanilla extract

1 lb softened cream cheese

1 c. berry preserves

Powdered sugar

Butter and vegetable oil for cooking

Extras

❧ Abbreviations and Basic Stitches ❧

BO: bind off

CC: contrast color (followed by # if more than one)

CO: cast on

K: knit

K#tog: knit designated number of stitches together

K1f&b: knit into front and back of same stitch

K1tbl: knit one stitch through the back loop

Kwise: as if to knit

LH: left hand

M1: make 1 increase

MC: main color

P: purl

P#tog: purl designated number of stitches together

Pm: place marker

Ptbl: purl through the back loop

Pwise: as if to purl

RH: right hand

RS: right side

Sk2p: slip 1 stitch, k2tog, pass slipped stitch over

Sl#: slip specified number of stitches without working them

Ssk: slip, slip, knit decrease

Ssp: slip, slip, purl decrease

WS: wrong side

Wr&t: wrap & turn for short row shaping (see *Basic Stitches*)

Wyif: with yarn in front

Wyib: with yarn in back

Yo: yarnover increase (yarn forward in UK)

Stockinette Stitch (worked in the round)
All rounds: Knit.

Garter Stitch (worked in the round)
Round 1: Knit.
Round 2: Purl.

1x1 Rib (in the round on an even number of stitches):
Round 1: *K1, p1; repeat from * to end.
Round 2 and all subsequent rounds: Knit the knit stitches and purl the purl stitches.

W&t (Wrap and turn)
On a RS row, work to point specified, slip the next stitch pwise from left to right hand needle, bring yarn to front of work, slip the stitch back to left hand needle, bring yarn around the stitch to back of work (wrapping the stitch). Turn work to WS.
On a WS row, work to point specified, slip the next stitch pwise from left to right hand needle, bring yarn to back of work, slip the stitch back to left hand needle, bring yarn around the stitch to front of work (wrapping the stitch). Turn work to RS.
For all, when working wrapped stitches, work wraps together with stitches. On a RS row, insert needle from front to back, into both the wrap and wrapped stitch and knit them together. On a WS row, insert needle from back to front, into both the wrap and wrapped stitch and purl them together.

Kitchener Stitch
Step 1: Bring threaded tapestry needle through first stitch on front needle as if to purl and leave stitch on needle.
Step 2: Bring threaded tapestry needle through first stitch on back needle as if to knit and leave stitch on needle.
Step 3: Bring threaded tapestry needle through first stitch on front needle as if to knit and slip this stitch off needle.
Step 4: Bring threaded tapestry needle through next stitch on front needle as if to purl and leave stitch on needle.
Step 5: Bring threaded tapestry needle through first stitch on back needle as if to purl and slip this stitch off needle.
Step 6: Bring threaded tapestry needle through next stitch on back needle as if to knit and leave stitch on needle.
Repeat steps 3–6 until no stitches remain on needles.

PlanetPurl.com Videos for this Book

Cast Ons
Judy's Magic Cast On
Knitted Cast On
Long Tail Cast On
Provisional Cast On
Turkish Cast On

Bind Offs
Picot Bind Off
Bind Off in Knit
Bind Off in Pattern
Sewn Ribbed Bind Off
Jeny's Suprisingly Stretchy Bind Off

Knit and Purl
1x1 Rib
Garter Stitch
Knit Stitch (American and Continental)
Knit Through Back Loop
Knitting in the Round on Two Circular Needles
Pick Up and Knit
Pick Up and Purl
Purl Stitch
Short Row Shaping
Slip Stitch with Yarn in Back/Front
Stockinette and Reverse Stockinette Stitch

Increases
Knit 1 Front & Back (k1f&b)
M1 Left Leaning
M1 Right Leaning
Yarnovers and Double Yarnovers

Decreases
Knit 2 Together (k2tog)
Purl 2 Together (p2tog)
Ssk: slip, slip, knit decrease
Skp: slip, knit, psso
Sk2p: slip, k2tog, psso

Lace Knitting
Blocking Lace
Knitting with Lifelines
Reading Lace Charts

Cable Knitting
Reading Cable Charts
Cable Front
Cable Back
Right Twist
Left Twist

Colorwork
Reading Color Charts
Knitting Jogless Stripes in the Round
Stranded (Fair Isle) Knitting
Intarsia Knitting

Finishing
Kitchener Stitch
Mattress Stitch
Satin Stitch
Spider Web Stitch

Free Online Classes
Beaded Knitting
Basic Lace Knitting
Cables & Twists
Intarsia
Toe-Up Socks

❦ Resources ❦

Knitting Fever, Inc.
www.KnittingFever.com

Lorna's Laces
www.LornasLaces.net

Berroco, Inc.
www.Berroco.com

Cascade Yarns
www.CascadeYarns.com

❖ Index ❖

DEEP SOUTH knitting

Beth Moriarty

25 Projects and 12 Recipes Inspired by America's Deep South

www.DeepSouthKnitting.com

Photo Credits

Page 7: Xiaoping Liang
Page 8: Laura Coles
Page 11: Denis Tangney
Page 15: Michael Gaffney
Page 19: Steve Greer
Page 23 (1): Aimain Tang
Page 23 (3): Christopher Penler
Page 25: Angela Schmidt
Page 30: Denis Tangney
Page 33: WerksMedia
Page 37 (1): Creative Commons
Page 37 (2): Skyhobo

Page 37 (3): Derek Dammann
Page 39: Josh Wickham
Page 43: Fotolinchen
Page 46: Antares71
Page 48: Ben Klaus
Page 51: Vasily Pindyurin
Page 52: Creative Commons
Page 57: Bryan Busovicki
Page 60: Lauri Patterson
Page 62: Tom Hahn
Page 65: Kimberly Deprey

Page 67 (1): Brad Boserup
Page 67 (2): Power of Forever Photography
Page 67 (3): Loretta Hostettler
Page 68: Seanicer
Page 70: Zack Schnepf
Page 73: Kacey Baxter
Page 77: Dan Moore
Page 83: Kavram
Page 87 (1): Rhonda Suka
Page 87 (2): Matthew Ragan
Page 87 (3): Dave Alan
Page 88: James Blinn

Notes

_____

_____

_____

_____

_____

_____

_____

_____

_____

_____